# Skill Sharpeners 3

## SECOND EDITION

Judy DeFilippo
Charles Skidmore

**ADDISON-WESLEY PUBLISHING COMPANY**

Reading, Massachusetts • Menlo Park, California
New York • Don Mills, Ontario • Wokingham, England
Amsterdam • Bonn • Sydney • Singapore • Tokyo • Madrid • San Juan

Judy DeFilippo is a coordinator of ESL in the Intensive English program at Northeastern University. She is author of *Lifeskills 1* and *2* and *Lifeskills and Citizenship,* and is co-author of *Grammar Plus,* all published by Addison-Wesley.

Charles Skidmore is an ESL teacher at the secondary level in the Boston, Massachusetts, schools and at Boston University's CELOP program. He is co-author of *In Good Company* also published by Addison-Wesley.

**A Publication of the World Language Division**

Editorial: Talbot Hamlin, Elly Schottman

Production/Manufacturing: James W. Gibbons

Illustrations: Kathleen Todd, Elizabeth Hazelton, publisher's files

Cover design: Marshall Henrichs, Richard Hannus

ISBN 0-201-51327-7

12 13 -PO- 01 00

# Introduction

The *Skill Sharpeners* series has been especially designed for students whose skills in standard English, especially those skills concerned with reading and writing, require strengthening. It is directed both toward students whose first language is not English and toward those who need additional practice in standard English grammar and vocabulary. By introducing basic skills tied to classroom subjects in a simple, easy-to-understand grammatical framework, the series helps to prepare these students for success in regular ("mainstream") academic subjects. By developing and reinforcing school and life survival skills, it helps build student confidence and self esteem.

This second edition of *Skill Sharpeners* not only updates the content of many pages, it also provides increased focus for some of the grammar exercises and adds new emphasis on higher order thinking skills. In addition, there are more content-area readings, more biographies, new opportunities for students to write, and more practice in using formats similar to those of many standardized tests. The central purpose of the series remains the same, however. *Skill Sharpeners* remains dedicated to helping your students sharpen their skills in all facets of English communication.

With English as a Second Language students, *Skill Sharpeners* supplements and complements any basic ESL text or series. With these students and with others, *Skill Sharpeners* can also be used to reteach and reinforce specific skills with which students are having—or have had—difficulty. In addition, it can be used to review and practice grammatical structures and to reinforce, expand, and enrich students' vocabularies.

The grammatical structures in the *Skill Sharpeners* series follow a systematic, small-step progression with many opportunities for practice, review, and reinforcement. Vocabulary and skill instruction is presented in the context of situations and concepts that have an immediate impact on students' daily lives. Themes and subject matter are directly related to curriculum areas. Reading and study skills are stressed in many pages, and writing skills are carefully developed, starting with single words and sentences and building gradually to paragraphs and stories in a structured, controlled composition sequence.

If you are using *Skill Sharpeners* with a basic text or series, you may find that the structural presentation in *Skill Sharpeners* deviates from that in your text. In such a case, you should not expect most of your students to be able actively to use the structures on some pages in speaking or writing. The students should, however, be able to read and respond to the content. Do not be concerned about structural errors during discussion of the material. It is important that students become *actively involved* and *communicating*, however imperfectly, from the very beginning.

# Using the *Skill Sharpeners*

Because each page or pair of pages of the *Skill Sharpeners* books is independent and self contained, the series lends itself to great flexibility of use. Teachers may pick and choose pages that fit the needs of particular students, or they may use the pages in sequential order. Most pages are self-explanatory, and all are easy to use, either in class or as homework assignments. Annotations at the bottom of each page identify the skill or skills being developed and suggest ways to prepare for, introduce, and present the exercise(s) on the page. In most cases, oral practice of the material is suggested before the student is asked to complete the page in writing. Teacher demonstration and student involvement and participation help build a foundation for completing the page successfully and learning the skill.

The *Skill Sharpeners* are divided into thematic units. The first unit of each book is introductory. In *Skill Sharpeners 1*, this unit provides exercises to help students say and write their names and addresses and to familiarize them with basic classroom language, school deportment, the names of school areas and school personnel, and number names. In later books of the series, the first unit serves both to review some of the material taught in earlier books and to provide orientation to the series for students coming to it for the first time.

At the end of each of the *Skill Sharpeners* books is a review of vocabulary and an end-of-book test of grammatical and reading skills. The test, largely in multiple-choice format, not only assesses learning of the skills but also provides additional practice for other multiple-choice tests.

The complete Table of Contents in each book identifies the skills developed on each page. A Skills Index at the end of the book lists skills alphabetically by topic and indicates the pages on which they are developed.

*Skill Sharpeners* invite expansion! We encourage you to use them as a springboard and to add activities and exercises that build on those in the books to fill the needs of your own particular students. Used this way, the *Skill Sharpeners* can significantly help to build the confidence and skills that students need to be successful members of the community and successful achievers in subject-area classrooms.

# Contents

## UNIT 4 Tasks and Travel

## UNIT 5 What About You?

## UNIT 6 People, Places, and Progress

## UNIT 10  Odds and Ends

## UNIT 11  Good, Better, Best

# Choose the Best Word

**Circle the best answer.** The first one is done for you.

1. I didn't see you last night. Where [ was / **were** ] you?

2. Robert can't [ find / found ] his shoes.

3. Does Kit Ming [ takes / take ] the bus to school?

4. Everyone [ was / were ] dancing and singing at the party.

5. I [ went / go ] to the dentist yesterday.

6. Did you [ like / liked ] the movie?

7. Jim is [ doing / does ] his homework now.

8. Are you [ rent / renting ] an apartment?

9. [ Do / Are ] you play volleyball?

10. I'm [ have / having ] a party tonight. Can you come?

11. Ronald likes [ ride / riding ] his bicycle to school.

12. [ Was / Were ] Minh in class yesterday?

13. Maria [ writes / writing ] to her grandmother every month.

14. [ Was / Were ] the teachers at a meeting yesterday?

15. The bus [ leaving / leaves ] at ten o'clock.

16. George didn't [ washed / wash ] the dishes.

**Skill Objective: Choosing the correct verb tense and form — simple present and past, present and past progressive.** This page may be used as a quick evaluation of the student's ability to distinguish and use the four verb tenses. Do the first example as a group activity, then assign the page as independent work. Students who find the page difficult should be grouped for reteaching. Analyze the type of mistakes being made and provide additional practice in these skills.

# Small Talk

**A. Complete each of these sentences.** This first one is done for you.

1. I'm going to the library because ___I want to take out some books.___
   _____

2. She has to walk to work because _____
   _____

3. The concert started late because _____
   _____

4. She didn't go to school because _____
   _____

5. The girls don't want to go to that movie because _____
   _____

6. We are driving to California because _____
   _____

7. We stopped at the supermarket because _____
   _____

8. We are going to a restaurant because _____
   _____

9. David is taking the train to Dallas because _____
   _____

**B. Read the following questions. Answer each question by making a check mark in the right box under *Yes, No,* or *Sometimes.***

| | Yes | No | Sometimes |
|---|---|---|---|
| 1. Do shirts have buttons? | | | |
| 2. Do shoes have zippers? | | | |
| 3. Do pants have sleeves? | | | |
| 4. Do pants have zippers? | | | |
| 5. Do men wear blouses? | | | |
| 6. Do belts go around the chest? | | | |
| 7. Do hats go on people's heads? | | | |
| 8. Do shirts have collars? | | | |
| 9. Do skirts have hems? | | | |
| 10. Do sweaters have pockets? | | | |

**Skill Objectives: Reviewing verb tenses; understanding cause and effect; building vocabulary; charting information.** Cover Part A as an oral group activity. Students should be as creative as possible and think up as many different reasons as they can for each item. *Part B:* Teach/review clothing vocabulary by giving directions: *If you are wearing a zipper, sit on your desk. If you are wearing more than four buttons, write your name on the board, etc.* Complete the first two items in Part B as a class, then assign the page as independent work.

# Likes and Dislikes

**Most people like to do some things and do not like to do others. Look at the pictures. Then write what the persons or animals like to do and what they don't like to do.** The first one is done for you. Use it as a model for the others.

1. *Samir likes playing baseball, but he doesn't like studying history.*

2. Carolina

3. Binh

4. Ed and Al

5. My cat

6. They

7. Elena

**Skill Objective: Using *like(s), doesn't/don't like* plus gerund.** Give several statements of likes/dislikes: *I like skiing, but I don't like skating. I like eating, but I don't like gaining weight.* Ask students, "How about you?" After four or five have volunteered, ask their classmates to recall their statements. *Alicia likes playing with babies, but she doesn't like changing them.* If students use the infinitive verb instead of the gerund ("likes to play"), praise the sentence as correct, and encourage students to use both forms for variety. Assign the page for written work.

**11**

# Interviewing:
# Getting To Know Each Other

**A. Make the following phrases into questions. Ask your classmates the questions. Ask your teacher, too. Try to find one person who can answer "yes." Write the person's name. Be sure to form the questions correctly.**

Example: *likes pizza:* "Do you like pizza?"                    Name

1. has the same number of brothers and sisters as you do    _____

2. is going to celebrate a birthday soon    _____

3. wants to have a big family someday (5 or more children)    _____

4. can play a musical instrument    _____

5. likes playing volleyball    _____

6. saw a movie last weekend    _____

7. would like to be a teacher someday    _____

8. knows who the principal (headmaster, director) of this school is    _____

9. is going to college someday    _____

10. was born in the same month as you    _____

**B. Write a paragraph about yourself. Use some of the same kinds of information as in the questions you asked. For example, tell when and where you were born, how many brothers and sisters you have, how large a family you want, and so on.**

_____

_____

_____

_____

_____

_____

_____

_____

_____

_____

**Skill Objectives: Interviewing; giving an oral report; asking questions; writing a paragraph.** Ask if anyone had a birthday recently or will have one soon. When is/was it? As responses are given, write them on the board: *Kim's birthday was yesterday, September 15; Juan's birthday is next week, September 20,* etc. Then have students practice asking when classmates' birthdays are. Ask other questions for oral practice, then tell students they are going to ask classmates the questions on the page and try to get at least one "yes" answer to each question. Have them record their answers and report to the class. *Part B:* Assign this for independent written work.

# Alternative Word Meanings

The dictionary often lists several meanings for one word. Read the following dictionary entries. **Decide which meaning of the word is being used in each sentence. Write the number of that definition in front of the sentence.** The first one is done for you.

**run**
1. to move rapidly
2. to take part in a race or election
3. to manage, be in charge of
4. to operate, work or move

  _3_   My father <u>runs</u> the supermarket on 12th Street.

  ____   Paul Lopez is going to <u>run</u> for class president.

  ____   There's my bus. I've got to <u>run</u>!

  ____   My car <u>runs</u> best on premium gas.

**note**
1. a musical sound
2. a short letter
3. reputation or fame

  ____   The song ended on a sweet <u>note</u>.

  ____   Jason's mother wrote his teacher a <u>note</u>.

  ____   Henry Larkin is a musician of some <u>note</u>.

**fly**
1. to move through the air with wings
2. to pass quickly
3. to wave in the air
4. to travel by aircraft

  ____   Paul Peterson, the reporter, has to <u>fly</u> to the West Coast often.
  ____   Most birds <u>fly</u> south for the winter.

  ____   Time does <u>fly</u> when you're having fun.

  ____   <u>Fly</u> the flag proudly, boys.

**poor**
1. needy, having too little money
2. unhappy, deserving pity
3. unsatisfactory, not good

  ____   Your <u>poor</u> performance on this test shows that you didn't study.

  ____   There are many <u>poor</u> people in this city.

  ____   Look at that <u>poor</u>, wet cat.

**carry**
1. to pick up and bring
2. to win
3. to hold up, support
4. to have for sale

  ____   Jose, can you <u>carry</u> these books downstairs, please?
  ____   This little wagon can <u>carry</u> over 100 pounds.
  ____   Did the Democrats <u>carry</u> this state in the last election?
  ____   This store doesn't <u>carry</u> calendars.

**Skill Objectives: Choosing the correct definition; building vocabulary.** Review the directions, then do the first set of sentences as a group activity. Assign the page as independent work. Extension Activity: Students can write sentences illustrating two or three different meanings of some of these words: *light, fair, block, hand, match, fall, figure, head*. They may use their dictionaries for help.

13

# 200 Years of American History

1775 ┬ 1775 Revolutionary War begins
     ├ 1776 Declaration of Indepen-
     │      dence
     │
     ├ 1787 Constitution written
     ├ 1789 Washington becomes first
     │      President
1800 ┤
     ├ 1803 Jefferson purchases
     │      Louisiana from France

1825 ┤
     ├ 1836 Texas becomes indepen-
     │      dent republic
     │
     ├ 1845 Texas joins the U.S.
     ├ 1846 Mexican-American War
1850 ┤      begins
     │
     ├ 1861 Civil War begins
     ├ 1865 Civil War ends
     ├ 1867 U.S. purchases Alaska
     ├ 1869 Railroads link east coast
     │      and west coast
1875 ┤
     │
     ├ 1898 Spanish-American War
1900 ┤
     │
     ├ 1917 U.S. enters World War I
     ├ 1920 Women allowed to vote
     │      nationwide
1925 ┤
     ├ 1929 Great Depression begins
     │
     ├ 1941 Pearl Harbor. U.S. enters
     │      World War II
     ├ 1945 World War II ends
1950 ┤
     ├ 1950 Korean War begins
     │
     ├ 1959 Alaska and Hawaii become
     │      states
     ├ 1961 U.S. enters Vietnam War
     │
     ├ 1969 U.S. puts first man on the
     │      moon
1975 ┴ 1975 Vietnam War ends

**Answer the following questions in complete sentences, using the time line to help you. Remember to write all your answers in the past tense.** The first one is done for you.

1. When did the U.S. enter the Vietnam War?

   *The U.S. entered the Vietnam War in 1961.*

   _____

2. When did Texas join the United States?

   _____

   _____

3. When did Thomas Jefferson purchase Louisiana from France?

   _____

   _____

4. When did Alaska and Hawaii become states?

   _____

   _____

5. When did women get the right to vote nationwide?

   _____

   _____

6. When did the Civil War begin?

   _____

   _____

7. When did the Great Depression begin?

   _____

   _____

8. When did Washington become president?

   _____

   _____

9. When did World War II end?

   _____

   _____

10. When did railroads link the east and west?

   _____

   _____

**Skill Objectives: Interpreting a time line; sequencing.** Have volunteers read the notations on the time line aloud. Help with reading dates and with vocabulary if necessary. Then go through the ten questions orally, having students answer in complete sentences. If students have additional knowledge about any of the events or places, encourage discussion. Have students complete the page independently. Remind them to write their answers in complete sentences.

# Affirmative and Negative

**A.** The time line on the facing page will show you that the following statements are "false." **Change these statements to "true" by changing the affirmative to the negative.** The first one is done for you.

1. The Civil War began in 1864. _The Civil War didn't begin in 1864._

2. Women were able to vote nationwide before 1920. _____

_____

3. George Washington purchased Louisiana from France. _____

_____

4. Texas became a state in 1845. _____

_____

5. The Civil War lasted ten years. _____

_____

6. The U.S.S.R. put the first man on the moon. _____

_____

7. The Korean War came before World War II. _____

_____

8. Thomas Jefferson was the first president of the United States. _____

_____

**B.** The following statements are answers to questions. **Write the question under each answer.** The first one is done for you.

1. George Washington became president in 1789.

   When _did George Washington become president_ ?

2. The Revolutionary War lasted for eight years.

   How long _____ ?

3. Alaska and Hawaii became states in 1959.

   When _____ ?

4. The United States entered World War II because the Japanese bombed Pearl Harbor.

   Why _____ ?

5. George Washington became president in 1789.

   When _____ ?

6. The Civil War began at Fort Sumter in South Carolina.

   Where _____ ?

7. Jefferson purchased the Louisiana Territory in 1803.

   What _____ ?

8. Texas was an independent republic from 1836 to 1845.

   How long _____ ?

**Skill Objectives: Forming negative sentences; asking questions.** Write on the board, *Alaska and Hawaii became states in 1969.* Ask if the sentence is true. Have students check the time line on the previous page for the answer (it's not true). Have students form the negative past: *Alaska and Hawaii didn't become . . .* Write, *When _____ ?* Have students form the correct past question form, *When did . . .?* answering orally. After a few more examples on the board, assign the page for independent work. As an option, you may wish to go through the whole page orally before assigning it for written work.

15

# More Than a Name

**A.** Make sure you know the meaning of the following important words which are underlined in the story.

| famous | ended | continued | mules | architecture |
| personalities | tobacco | talented | foreign | designed |

**B.** Read the story quickly to get some general ideas about it. Then read it again more slowly to answer the questions.

## Our First Three Presidents

Many times when people study history, they learn a few facts about the famous names that they see in their text books, but they don't learn about the personalities of these famous people. For example, every student of American history knows that George Washington, John Adams, and Thomas Jefferson were the first three Presidents of the United States, but what else do they know about these interesting men?

George Washington was a quiet man. He liked to hunt and fish. He liked to give parties, but he also liked to go to bed early. His parties always ended at 9:00. After George Washington was President, he lived on his farm. He liked planting tobacco and raising mules.

John Adams was a bright and serious man. He liked to study law and history. After he was President, he returned to his home in Massachusetts. He continued to study. He liked to write about politics. He wrote many famous letters to the next president, Thomas Jefferson.

Thomas Jefferson, the third president, was a very talented man. In some ways he was like George Washington. He liked living on a farm, and he liked riding horses and hunting. Thomas Jefferson had other interests, too. He liked to play the violin, and he liked to sing. He liked speaking foreign languages, and he learned Latin, Greek, Italian, French, and Spanish. After Jefferson was President, he returned to one of his other interests, architecture. He designed the buildings for the University of Virginia.

Now you know a little more about the first three Presidents. When you are studying history, remember that the people in the books are more than names. Don't be afraid to go to the library and find out more about their personalities.

**C.** Think carefully and answer the following question.

According to the story, what was George Washington most probably doing by 10:00 at night?

a. having a party  
c. sleeping  

b. writing letters  
d. planting tobacco

(Go on to the next page.)

**Skill Objectives: Reading comprehension; building vocabulary.** Review the directions with the students. After the first reading, you may wish to lead a discussion about the meaning of the highlighted vocabulary words. Encourage students to check and refine their definitions by using a dictionary.

**D. What is the main idea of the story? Circle the best answer.**

1. Washington, Adams, and Jefferson were our first three Presidents.

2. Washington, Adams, and Jefferson had many different interests.

3. Washington, Adams, and Jefferson went home after they were President.

4. Washington, Adams, and Jefferson are famous names.

**E. Use a word from the underlined vocabulary to complete each of these sentences.**

1. Pierre can sing, dance, and play the piano. He's very _____.

2. Everybody knows James Bond; he's a _____ character.

3. The party started at 8:00 and _____ at 12:30.

4. I don't understand these words; they are in a _____ language.

5. The music stopped for a moment and then _____.

**F. Answer these questions on another piece of paper.**

1. Who were the first three Presidents of the United States?
2. Why did George Washington's parties end at 9:00?
3. What did George Washington like to do on his farm?
4. What did John Adams like to study?
5. Where did John Adams live?
6. How were Thomas Jefferson and George Washington alike?
7. What foreign languages did Thomas Jefferson learn?
8. What did Thomas Jefferson do at the University of Virginia?

**G. Complete this outline of the story by filling in details.**

A. Things George Washington liked to do.

1. _____

2. _____

3. _____

B. Things John Adams liked to do.

1. _____

2. _____

3. _____

C. Things Thomas Jefferson liked to do.

1. _____

2. _____

3. _____

**Skill Objectives: Identifying main idea and details; building vocabulary; outlining.** Students should complete these exercises independently. Correct and discuss the page as a class. Extension Activity: Interested students can use the encyclopedia to find out facts about the childhood of these three Presidents. They should write down these facts in outline form. Remind students to skim each article, using the headings, to find the section that deals specifically with that President's early life.

**17**

# A Busy Morning

**A. Look at the picture story of Jane's morning. Use it to fill in the blanks in the paragraph below.** The first one is done for you.

Jane got up late yesterday morning. She ran _____*to*_____ the bathroom, brushed

her _____ , and washed her face. Then she _____ into the kitchen and

looked in _____ refrigerator. She decided to have _____ only because she

was late. While she _____ drinking her coffee, she quickly _____ the

morning newspaper. After breakfast, she _____ dressed, left her apartment,

_____ ran to the bus stop. Unfortunately, _____ missed the bus and had to

_____ for the next.

**B. Now read each of the statements below and look at the picture story. Write *T* if the statement is true. Write *F* if the statement is false. Write *?* if the story does not give you enough information to decide if the statement is true or false.** The first one is done for you.

___*?*___ 1. Jane got up at 8:00 yesterday.

_____ 2. She brushed her teeth before breakfast.

_____ 3. She had a large breakfast.

_____ 4. She got dressed before breakfast.

_____ 5. She hurried to the bus stop.

_____ 6. She waited fifteen minutes for the bus.

---

**Skill Objectives: Using pictures to complete a story; distinguishing between true, false, and ?.** Have students look at the picture story and tell you what Jane did yesterday. *Part A:* Explain that one word is missing from each blank and students are to fill in that word. There may be more than one correct answer for any blank: *into* would be as correct as *to* for the first one. Explain that students must follow the pictures to fill in the blanks. If necessary, go through the exercise orally before assigning it for written work. *Part B:* Be sure students understand when to use the ?: Jane may or may not have gotten up at 8, but the story doesn't tell us.

**18**

# Word Skills: Homophones

Some words in English sound exactly alike but have different spellings and meanings. These words are called *homophones.* Here are some examples of homophones.

**He ate eight eggs.**    **She rode down the road.**    **My son is playing in the sun.**

**Complete the following sentences. Use the words in the Data Bank.** Your dictionary will help you choose the correct homophone. The first one is done for you.

1. He is a vegetarian; he doesn't eat ____*meat*____.

2. Mei Lee knows how to _____ her own clothes.

3. There are sixty minutes in one _____.

4. Yesterday, there was a big _____ at the department store.

5. The Sampsons are going to visit _____ daughter.

6. Sonia traveled to California by _____.

7. Hanibal is shopping; he wants a new _____ of shoes.

8. Everyone wants to go _____ the movies tonight.

9. Speak a little louder please. I can't _____ you.

10. Please _____ here until the boys come out.

11. The Turners are going to _____ a new car.

12. Walk to the end of the street and turn _____.

13. The girls _____ the answer, but I don't.

14. Rita received three letters in today's _____.

15. The students stayed in New York last _____.

16. James punched Peter in the _____ this morning.

## D A T A  B A N K

| | | | |
|---|---|---|---|
| by, buy, bye | meat, meet | plane, plain | their, there, they're |
| eye, I | no, know | right, write | to, two, too |
| here, hear | our, hour | sail, sale | wait, weight |
| mail, male | pear, pair, pare | so, sew | weak, week |

**Skill Objective: Distinguishing between homophones.** Review the definition of homophones and go over the three illustrated examples with the class. Complete several items as a group, then assign the page as independent work. Extension Activity: Encourage students to use the homophones in the Data Bank to write sentences similar to the three at the top of this page. Each sentence should contain two or more homophones. Example: *I feel weak this week.*

## Dear Dot

Dear Dot—

Last week I was playing tennis with my boyfriend, Jimmy. We played three matches, and I was the winner every time. Jimmy was very angry. He said he was never going to play tennis with me again. I like tennis because it is such good exercise. How can I convince Jimmy to continue playing tennis with me?

Chrissy

1. When were Chrissy and Jimmy playing tennis? _____

_____

2. How many matches did they play? _____

3. Why do you think Jimmy was angry? _____

_____

4. What did Jimmy say to Chrissy? _____

_____

5. Why does Chrissy like to play tennis? _____

_____

6. What does the word *convince* mean as used in this letter? Circle the best answer.

   a. beat      b. bother      c. bring      d. talk into

7. What is your advice to Chrissy? Discuss your answer in class. Then read Dot's answer, and tell why you agree or disagree. Dot's advice is below.

Dear Chrissy—

Try talking to Jimmy. Does he really want you not to play just as well as you can? Does he really think that men have to be superior to women? If he does (or you think that he does) find another tennis partner. And think about Jimmy's attitude before you get too serious with him.

Dot

**Skill Objectives: Reading comprehension; understanding words through context; making judgments.** Have students read the letter and answer the questions independently. If you wish, have students write their advice to Chrissy on a separate piece of paper. Correct the page as a class, then have students compare and discuss their own advice and Dot's reply. You may want to raise these questions for discussion: "Why do you think Jimmy got angry?" "How do you think Jimmy would have acted if he had lost the match to another boy?"

# Sensible Sam

Sam tries to be sensible about eating. This chart shows some of the things he does. **Look at the chart, and then follow the instructions below it.**

| | Always | Usually | Sometimes | Seldom | Never |
|---|---|---|---|---|---|
| 1. Eats a good breakfast | X | | | | |
| 2. Has a bowl of cereal with fruit | | X | | | |
| 3. Has two scrambled eggs | | | X | | |
| 4. Drinks cola for breakfast | | | | | X |
| 5. Brings lunch to school | | | X | | |
| 6. Buys lunch in cafeteria | | | X | | |
| 7. Skips lunch | | | | X | |
| 8. Eats dinner with his family at 6:30 | X | | | | |
| 9. Helps in the kitchen after dinner | | X | | | |

**A. Use the chart to write about Sam.** The first two sentences are done for you.

*Sam tries to eat sensibly. He always eats a good breakfast.*

_____

_____

_____

_____

_____

_____

**B. Now write about you. Use *always, usually, sometimes, seldom, never.***

_____

_____

_____

_____

_____

_____

**Skill Objectives: Adverbs of frequency; interpreting a chart.** Read the introductory lines aloud, then ask questions about the chart. *What does Sam (always, hardly ever, etc.) do? Does Sam (always) bring lunch to school?* Encourage students to ask each other similar questions. Assign the page for independent work. Extension Activity: Have students write about their daily schedules, using each adverb of frequency at least once. These questions may help focus their thoughts: *When do you get up? What do you do before/after school? What do you do at night?*

# Counting Calories

A calorie is a measure of the energy you get from food. If the food you eat supplies more calories than you use up, you gain weight. If it supplies fewer calories than you use up, you lose weight. The tables below show how many calories are in some foods many Americans eat for breakfast, lunch, and dinner.

| Breakfast | Calories |
|---|---|
| orange juice (1 cup) | 110 |
| 1 fried egg | 95 |
| boiled egg | 80 |
| whole wheat toast | 55 |
| 1 pat butter | 50 |
| 2 slices bacon | 90 |
| coffee | |
| 1 tsp. whole milk | 20 |
| 1 tsp. sugar | 18 |
| cup coffee/skim milk | 0 |

| Lunch | Calories |
|---|---|
| hamburger (4 oz.) | 320 |
| roll | 120 |
| 1 can of cola (12 oz.) | 150 |
| French fries (1 cup) | 570 |
| 1 banana | 95 |
| tomato juice (½ cup) | 25 |
| tuna salad (½ cup) | 180 |
| 1 slice Syrian bread | 80 |
| 1 medium apple | 75 |
| 1 can of diet cola (12 oz.) | 1 |

| Dinner | Calories |
|---|---|
| fried chicken (6 oz.) | 520 |
| broiled chicken (6 oz.) | 320 |
| 1 boiled potato | 125 |
| 1 cup peas | 120 |
| 1 slice French bread | 120 |
| 1 cup squash | 100 |
| 3 pats butter | 150 |
| 1 cup whole milk | 175 |
| 1 cup skim milk | 75 |
| 1 cup gelatin dessert | 140 |

## A. Use the tables to complete these sentences.

1. One slice of bacon has _____ calories.

2. Syrian bread has (more, fewer) calories than whole wheat bread. (Circle one.)

3. There are _____ more calories in a cup of whole milk than in a cup of skim milk.

4. Six ounces of broiled chicken has _____ fewer calories than six ounces of fried chicken.

5. There are _____ calories in one cup of tomato juice.

6. An apple has _____ fewer calories than a banana.

7. A hamburger, including the roll, has _____ calories.

8. A can of regular cola has _____ more calories than a can of diet cola.

9. A fried egg has _____ more calories than a boiled egg.

10. Two bananas have _____ calories.

11. A breakfast of a boiled egg, one slice of whole wheat toast, ½ pat of butter, and ½ cup of orange juice has _____ calories.

12. A breakfast of a fried egg, one slice of bacon, one slice of whole wheat toast, and a cup of black coffee has _____ calories.

13. A tuna salad (½ cup) sandwich on whole wheat bread has _____ calories.

## B. Susan's doctor says she must go on a diet of 1200 calories a day. **On your own paper, write a nutritious breakfast, lunch, and dinner for Susan with no more than 1200 calories. Use foods from the tables above.**

**Skill Objectives: Using charts to solve word problems; devising a diet.** Read the sentences at the top of the page with the class and give students time to look at the charts. Answer any questions about them. *Part A:* Do several items orally with the class, and be sure students understand how to use the charts to answer the questions. Assign for independent work. *Part B:* Call on volunteers to plan a sample nutritious breakfast for Susan. Then have students do plans for lunch and dinner. Remind them that all three meals must add up to no more than 1200 calories. The meals should include meats (or fish, dairy), fruits and vegetables, and bread.

# In the Kitchen (1)

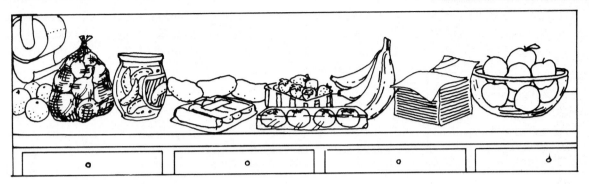

**Look at the picture of the kitchen counter. Use it to answer the questions. Where the answers are given, make up questions to go with them.** The first three are done for you.

1. Are there any apples in this kitchen?    *Yes, there are many.*

2. Are there any pears in this kitchen?    *No, there aren't any. (or "are none")*

3. Are there any oranges in this kitchen?    *Yes, there are some. (or "a few")*

4. Are there any cookies in this kitchen?    _____

5. Are there any napkins?    _____

6. Are there any bananas?    _____

7. Are there any eggs?    _____

8. Are there any lemons?    _____

9. Are there any sandwiches for lunch?    _____

10. Are there any pickles?    _____

11. Are there any tomatoes?    _____

12. Are there any lamb chops?    _____

13. Are there any paper towels?    _____

14. _____?  Yes, there are a few.

15. _____?  No, there aren't any.

16. _____?  Yes, there are many.

17. _____?  No, there are none.

18. How many hot dog rolls are there?    _____

19. How many hot dogs are there?    _____

20. How many potatoes are there?    _____

**Skill Objectives: Asking/answering questions—*Are there any . . .? How many . . .?*; using adverbs of quantity.** Write on the board: *Are there any . . .? How many . . . are there? (many, quite a few, some, a few, none/aren't any)* Teach/review the adverbs of quantity. Have students use the two question forms to ask each other about the number of items in the picture. Be sure students understand that the questions can also be answered with an exact number. After sufficient oral practice, assign the page for independent work.

**23**

# In the Kitchen (2)

Mr. Garcia has come back from the supermarket and is putting away the things he bought. **Look at the picture and answer the questions about Mr. Garcia's groceries. Where the answers are given, make up questions to go with them.** The first three are done for you.

1. Is there any corn? — *Yes, there is a lot.*

2. Is there any tuna fish? — *No, there isn't any. (or "is none")*

3. Is there any lettuce? — *Yes, there is some. (or "a little")*

4. Is there any orange juice? _____

5. Is there any sugar? _____

6. Is there any soap? _____

7. Is there any bread? _____

8. Is there any bacon? _____

9. Is there any ketchup? _____

10. Is there any salad oil? _____

11. Is there any cereal? _____

12. Is there any toothpaste? _____

13. Is there any cake? _____

14. _____? Yes, there is some.

15. _____? No, there isn't any.

16. How much soup is there? _____

17. How much rice is there? _____

18. How much butter is there? _____

**Skill Objective: Asking/answering quantity questions with non-count nouns.** Write: *Is there any . . .? How much . . . is there?* Teach the adverbs of quantity: *a lot, quite a lot, some, a little, none/isn't any.* Have students ask/answer questions about the picture. Draw a ¼-filled ketchup bottle, a stack of soap, two eggs and ten oranges. Ask, *How much ketchup/soap is there? How many eggs/oranges are there? (a litte, a lot; a few, many)* Note the different adverbs used with count vs. non-count nouns.

24

# Tony's Place

OPEN 7 DAYS   6 A.M.–11 P.M. MON.–FRI.   9 A.M.–11 P.M. SAT. & SUN.

## –SUBS–

| | SM. LG. | | SM. LG. | | SM. LG. |
|---|---|---|---|---|---|
| Cold Cuts | 3.15 3.60 | Tuna Salad | 3.55 3.95 | Sliced Turkey | 3.55 3.95 |
| Roast Beef | 3.55 3.95 | Bologna-Cheese | 3.15 3.60 | Salami-Cheese | 3.55 3.95 |
| Ham & Cheese | 3.15 3.60 | Crabmeat | 3.55 3.95 | Chicken Salad | 3.55 3.95 |

### –Try the hot ones–

| | SM. LG. | | SM. LG. | | SM. LG. |
|---|---|---|---|---|---|
| Steak | 3.55 3.95 | Sausage | 3.15 3.60 | Meatball | 3.15 3.60 |
| Steak-Peppers | 3.55 3.95 | Sausage & Meatball | 3.55 3.95 | Ham-Egg | 3.15 3.60 |
| Steak-Onions | 3.55 3.95 | Veal Cutlet | 3.15 3.60 | Hamburger | 2.60 3.00 |

### –PIZZA WITH PIZZAZZ–   Buy 3 Pizzas—Get One Free

| | SM. LG. | | SM. LG. | | SM. LG. |
|---|---|---|---|---|---|
| Cheese | 3.70 6.95 | Sausage | 4.30 8.20 | Ham | 4.30 8.20 |
| Onion | 4.30 8.20 | Pepperoni | 4.30 8.20 | Bacon | 4.50 8.45 |
| Pepper | 4.30 8.20 | Mushroom | 4.30 8.45 | Any 2 Combo | 5.00 8.90 |

**Pizza Served Mon.–Thurs. 5–11 P.M.   Fri.–Sun. 4–11 P.M.**

| BEVERAGES | | | | SIDE SPECIALS | | |
|---|---|---|---|---|---|---|
| | | | | **Salads** | | |
| Soda | .70 | Coffee | .60  .80 | | | |
| Milk | .55 | Tea | .60  .80 | French Fries | Garden | 3.95 |
| Juice | .75 | | | 1.25   1.75 | Greek | 4.50 |
| | | | | | Tuna | 4.80 |

**Look at Tony's menu. Use your dictionary for words you do not know.** (You may not find *sub*. It is a kind of sandwich made with a loaf of French bread that is split from end to end, and it has different names in different parts of the country.) **Now answer the questions about Tony's menu. Use short answers.**

1. Why are there two prices for each sub? _____

    _____

2. How much is a large steak and onion sub? _____

3. What are cold cuts? _____

4. How much is a small cold cut sub with a small order of French fries? _____

5. "Combo" stands for combination. What do you think a combo pizza is ? _____

    _____

6. How much is a small pizza with onions and peppers? _____

7. Merle bought four pizzas. How many did she have to pay for? _____

8. Can you buy a pizza for lunch at Tony's? _____

9. Is a large pepperoni pizza the same price as a large mushroom pizza? _____

10. How much is a Greek salad and a can of orange juice? _____

11. Is Tony's Place open every day? _____

12. You are picking up lunch for some friends. How much is a small chicken salad sub, a large meatball sub, a tuna salad, a small sliced turkey sub, a garden salad, and five sodas? _____

13. How much will you pay for three small tuna subs and two large coffees? _____

14. Do they probably sell cola at Tony's Place? _____

**Skill Objectives: Interpreting a menu; solving mathematical word problems.** Explain any unfamiliar words on the menu. Ask various students, *What would you like for lunch?* ("I'd like . . .") Prompt with additional questions, *Is that a large or a small (sub)? What would you like to drink?* Write the order on the board. Have the class compute the bill. Assign the page for independent work. Extension Activity: Have students role play ordering lunch at Tony's Place, paying their bill, and leaving a tip.

25

# Food for Your Health

**A.** Make sure you know the meaning of the following important words which are under-lined in the story.

necessary          major          poultry          prevent
health             specific       digest           bleeding

**B.** Read the story quickly to get some general ideas about it. Then read it again more slowly to answer the questions.

### Vitamins

Vitamins are <u>necessary</u> for good <u>health</u>. We get vitamins from the foods that we eat. There are about ten <u>major</u> vitamins. Each vitamin has a <u>specific</u> job to do in the body. Read about vitamins below.

- Vitamin A—Vitamin A comes from green and yellow vegetables. It is also in milk and egg yolks. Vitamin A is necessary for night vision, seeing in the dark.

- Vitamin $B_1$—Vitamin $B_1$ comes from fish, brown rice, and <u>poultry</u>. It is also in most meats and nuts. The job of vitamin $B_1$ is to build the blood and help the body <u>digest</u> food.

- Vitamin $B_{12}$—Vitamin $B_{12}$ comes from cheese, fish, and milk. The job of vitamin $B_{12}$ is to build up the red blood cells and to keep the body's nervous system healthy.

- Vitamin C—Vitamin C comes from citrus fruits such as oranges and grapefruit and other fruits such as strawberries. It is also in green peppers. Vitamin C is important in building bones and teeth, and some people say it helps to <u>prevent</u> colds.

- Vitamin D—Vitamin D comes from egg yolks. In the United States, the dairy industry also adds it to milk. People also get vitamin D from sunlight. Vitamin D is important for building strong bones.

- Vitamin E—Vitamin E comes from dark green vegetables such as spinach. It is also found in eggs and liver. Vitamin E is important in reproduction and muscle development.

- Vitamin K—Vitamin K comes from green leafy vegetables and yogurt. Its job is to help the blood to clot. Without vitamin K, cuts and scrapes keep <u>bleeding</u>. Vitamin K helps the cut to close. It keeps the body from losing too much blood.

**C.** Think carefully and answer the following question.
According to the article, which of the following is most likely to contain Vitamin A?
a. rice          b. liver          c. oranges          d. broccoli

(Go on the next page.)

**Skill Objectives: Reading comprehension; drawing conclusions; building vocabulary.** Review the directions with the students. After the first reading, you may wish to lead a discussion about the meaning of the highlighted vocabulary. Encourage students to check and refine their understanding of the words by using a dictionary.

**D. Circle the answer that best completes the sentence.**

Vitamins are necessary for good health because

    a. they are found in certain foods.
    b. they have important jobs to do in the body.
    c. there are ten major vitamins.
    d. they are chemical substances.

**E. Use a word from the underlined vocabulary to complete each of these sentences.**

1. Quick, get a bandage! Diana is _____.

2. Smoking is the _____ cause of lung cancer.

3. I don't understand your problem; please be more _____.

4. Don't let accidents happen; try to _____ them.

5. Most people agree that you can't be happy without your _____.

**F. Use separate paper to write answers to these questions. (Number your answers to match the questions.)**

1. What are three vitamins that come from green vegetables?
2. What vitamin does brown rice contain?
3. What vitamin do both egg yolks and sunlight provide?
4. What vitamin helps keep the nervous system healthy?
5. What vitamin helps blood to clot?
6. What does "clot" mean?
7. What fruits give us a good supply of vitamin C?
8. What foods give us a good supply of vitamin E?
9. What vitamin helps the body to digest food?
10. What is night vision?

**G. Look at the list of foods below. They have lots of vitamins. Are they part of your diet (what you eat)? Complete the chart by checking if you eat *lots of, some,* or *none* of each of the foods on the list.**

| | Lots of | Some | None |
|---|---|---|---|
| liver | | | |
| milk | | | |
| eggs | | | |
| fish | | | |
| nuts | | | |
| poultry | | | |
| green vegetables | | | |
| fruits | | | |
| rice | | | |

# Beginnings and Endings

**Find the right ending for each sentence, and write its letter in the blank. Each letter may be used only once.** The first one is done for you.

1. Lisa always studies, so __j__

2. Pablo always gets up late, so ____

3. Chang never eats breakfast, so ____

4. Mr. Watson seldom drives his car, so ____

5. The baby usually sleeps in the afternoon, so ____

6. Luis is always smiling, so ____

7. Peter frequently drives fast, so ____

8. Dulce doesn't know what's happening in the world because____

9. My little sister sometimes gets sick because ____

10. Wanda's boss is very angry at her because ____

11. Jill doesn't buy much at the cafeteria because ____

12. All the students want Mei Ling on their team because ____

13. Mr. Fell's students study hard every Thursday night because ____

14. Because it usually rains on weekends, ____

15. Because that store closes at 5:00, ____

16. Because Michael almost never eats sugar, ____

17. Because my uncle seldom writes letters, ____

18. Because English often is confusing, ____

19. Because the students sometimes are noisy, ____

20. Because my father always plays chess at my uncle's house on Friday night, ____

a. he's very hungry at lunch.

b. she always hits a home run.

c. we stay inside on Saturday and Sunday.

d. we have to be quiet when we get home from school.

e. the teacher has to tell them to be quiet.

f. he get a lot of tickets.

g. his teeth are in good condition.

h. she eats too much.

i. you have to shop early.

j. she gets good grades on her report card.

k. we call him on the phone every month.

l. she usually brings her lunch.

m. people are glad to see him.

n. he comes home late.

o. he often misses his first class.

p. you have to study it very carefully.

q. she almost never watches the news on TV.

r. he gives tests on Friday.

s. it is in good condition.

t. she often misses work.

---

**Skill Objectives: Noting cause and effect; using *so, because*.** Write on the board: *Lisa always studies, so she gets good grades. Lisa gets good grades because she always studies. Because she always studies, Lisa gets good grades.* Let students agree that all three sentences mean the same. Assign the page as written work. Extension Activity: Have students complete these sentences: *Angela didn't feel well, so . . . . Because I missed the last bus home . . . My father doesn't like winter because . . .*

# Word Skills: Antonyms

Antonyms are words that are opposite in meaning. *High* and *low* are antonyms because high is the opposite of low. Not every word has an antonym, but many do. Here are some common English antonyms. **Read the list and then answer the questions under it.**

| | | | |
|---|---|---|---|
| always/never | clean/dirty | right/left | before/after |
| often/seldom | open/close | in/out | big/little |
| question/answer | dead/alive | start/finish | day/night |
| arrive/leave | east/west | stop/go | near/far |
| awake/asleep | first/last | on/off | hello/goodbye |
| begin/end | front/back | up/down | hot/cold |
| buy/sell | love/hate | | |

1. Which antonym pair describes what people do in a store? _____

2. Which antonym pair describes directions on a map? _____

3. Which antonym pair describes a race? _____

4. Which antonym pair describes a red light and a green light? _____

5. Which antonym pair describes strong emotions? _____

6. Which antonym pair describes the weather? _____

7. Which antonym pair describes an elephant and an ant? _____

8. Which antonym pair describes sunlight and moonlight? _____

9. Which antonym pair describes a school test? _____

10. Which antonym pair describes out of bed or in bed? _____

11. Which antonym pair describes distances? _____

12. Which antonym pair describes car turn signals? _____

13. Which antonym pair describes stairways? _____

14. Which antonym pair describes a fast conversation? _____

15. Which antonym pair describes an electrical appliance? _____

16. Which antonym pair describes what a train does? _____

17. Which antonym pair describes the two covers of a book? _____

18. Which antonym pair describes what you do to a door? _____

**Skill Objectives: Understanding antonyms; classifying.** Say the following words, and have the class name the opposites: *yes, fat, early, young, win, empty, fast, wet, happy, summer, wonderful, tall, pretty.* Read the directions with the class and have students read the list of antonyms. Then assign the page as independent work. Discuss the answers as a class.

29

# Call the Doctor!

Most people are healthy most of the time, but now and then people do not feel well. Some people have serious illnesses or conditions, some have temporary sicknesses that are less serious, and some have diseases that they have "caught" from other people. Look at the three lists below. Use your dictionary or an encyclopedia to find out about each of the items on the lists.

| Illness/Condition | Sickness | Communicable Diseases |
|---|---|---|
| diabetes | flu (virus) | chicken pox |
| heart trouble | fever | German measles |
| cancer | headache, earache, | measles |
| tuberculosis | backache, etc. | mumps |
| allergy | upset stomach | scarlet fever |
| asthma | diarrhea | |

**A. Look at the list of conditions at the left. Draw a line from each condition to the symptoms (the way you feel or the effects of the condition) at the right.** The first one is done for you. Use your dictionary or an encyclopedia to help you.

1. headache
2. allergy
3. chicken pox
4. fever
5. upset stomach
6. diabetes
7. heart trouble
8. flu

a. you have a temperature of 102°F
b. you feel like throwing up your food
c. your body can't use sugar and you need insulin shots
d. you have a headache, sore throat, fever, earache, and cold
e. you sneeze from dust, flowers, and animals
f. children get red spots on their bodies
g. your heart is weak
h. your head hurts

**B.** Different kinds of doctors take care of different kinds of diseases or conditions. **Use words from the Data Bank to complete each of these sentences.** Use your dictionary if you need to.

1. When a woman is going to have a baby, she goes to a(n) _____.

2. When the baby is born, she takes it to a(n) _____.

3. A family doctor who treats common illnesses is a(n) _____.

4. If you have a toothache, you go to a(n) _____.

5. If you have to have your appendix removed, you go to a(n) _____.

6. If you are having trouble with your eyes, you go to a(n) _____.

7. People who are feeling depressed can go to a(n) _____.

## D A T A  B A N K

| | | | |
|---|---|---|---|
| dentist | general practitioner | obstetrician | ophthalmologist |
| pediatrician | psychiatrist | surgeon | |

**C. On your paper, write the names of other kinds of doctors and tell what they do. Use an encyclopedia to find this information.**

*Skill Objectives: Building vocabulary; discussing illnesses and symptoms.* Read the introduction with the class. Have students study the charts, using a dictionary when needed. Discuss the symptoms of the different ailments and how each illness can be treated. Ask students which illnesses they have had. Assign Parts A and B for independent or pair work. Part C may be done as homework. A group list of the names and descriptions of medical specialists can then be compiled.

# Follow the Directions

When you take any kind of medicine, it is important to follow the directions for that medicine. Your medicine may be either something prescribed by a doctor and supplied to you by a pharmacist in a drugstore or something that anyone can buy from a drugstore counter.

**A.** When a doctor believes you need a special kind of medicine, he or she writes a *prescription*. You take the prescription to the pharmacist who gives you the medicine. The label on the container tells you what the medicine is and how often you should take it.

**Look at this label. Use it to answer the questions.**

```
STONE PHARMACY
Jason Stone, Reg. Pharm.
Tel. 898-0225


No. 806-943      Date 7/2/91


Catherine Cook        Pen VK
                      250 mg

One tablet every 4 hours.


                      Dr. Morton
```

1. Who is the medicine for? _____

2. Is Jason Stone the doctor or the pharmacist? _____

3. What is the number of the prescription? _____

4. Pen VK is penicillin. What is penicillin? _____

5. Is Pen VK a liquid? _____

6. How often does Catherine have to take her medicine? _____

7. What is the name of the drugstore? _____

**B.** Most medicines that you buy from the drugstore counter have directions on the container. **Look at this set of directions from an aspirin bottle and use it to answer the questions.**

1. Why do people take aspirin? _____

_____

2. What is the recommended adult dosage?

_____

> Aspirin is used for relief of simple headache and for temporary relief of minor arthritic pain, the discomfort and fever of colds or "flu," menstrual cramps, muscular aches from fatigue, and toothache. Dosage: 2 tablets every four hours as needed. Do not exceed 12 tablets in 24 hours unless directed by physician. For children 6–12, one-half dose. Under 6, consult physician. **Warning: Keep this and all medicines out of children's reach. In case of accidental overdose, consult physician immediately. Caution:** If pain persists for more than 10 days or redness is present or in arthritic or rheumatic conditions affecting children under 12, consult a physician immediately. Do not take without consulting a physician if under medical care. Consult a dentist for toothache promptly. **Active ingredient:** Aspirin, 5 gr.
> STORE AT ROOM TEMPERATURE

3. What is the recommended dosage for children aged 6 to 12?

_____

4. What should parents of a child under 6 do before they give their child aspirin?

_____

5. Should you keep this bottle in the refrigerator? _____

**Skill Objective: Reading medical prescriptions and labels.** Read the introductory paragraphs together, then assign the page as independent work. Extension Activity: As a homework assignment, have students go to a drugstore and write down the names and uses of five non-prescription drugs or health products. Have students bring in their lists to share with the class. Students may wish to discuss ways of treating health problems other than using these products.

31

## Dear Dot

Dear Dot—

My son, Ronald, never goes out. He comes home from school and changes his clothes, and then he practices the piano. He plays for hours. After dinner he does his homework, and then he goes right back to his music. He doesn't have any friends. He never watches TV, and he never goes to the movies. Is he all right? I worry about him.

Concerned Mother

1. What does Ronald do after he changes his clothes? _____

   _____

2. What does Ronald do when he isn't playing the piano? _____

   _____

3. Is Ronald a popular person? _____

4. What do you think Concerned Mother wants Ronald to do? _____

   _____

5. What is the best meaning of *concerned,* as used in this letter? Circle your answer.

   a. late     b. worried     c. strong     d. angry

6. What is your advice to Concerned Mother? Discuss your answer in class. Then read Dot's answer and tell why you agree or disagree. Dot's advice is below.

Dear Mom—

It's easy to understand why you are concerned about Ronald. I agree that he doesn't behave the way most boys of his age do. He is completely involved in music and his own small world. However, if he wants to make his living as a musician, he needs to practice, practice, and practice. You can't and shouldn't try to force a social life on him (or on anyone). What you can do is encourage him, show your interest, and be ready to listen if he wants to share his thoughts and concerns. If you just want him to go out once in a while, why not get tickets to a concert or musical show and take him out as a special treat. But be sure it's his kind of music!

Dot

## Write About It

**On your paper, write a paragraph describing your typical day. Tell what you do from the time you get up until you go to bed.**

**Skill Objectives: Reading for details; drawing conclusions; understanding words through context; making judgments.** Have students read the letter and answer the questions independently. Students can write their advice to "Concerned Mother" on a separate piece of paper. Correct the first five questions as a class, then have students compare and discuss their own advice and Dot's reply. You may wish to assign the "Write About It" topic as homework.

# Summer Jobs

Look at these advertisements for summer jobs. Use them to answer the questions.

---

**YARD WORK**
Mon, Wed, Fri afternoons. $5.50/ hr. to start. Mowing, gardening, gen. maintenance. Call 332-0066 for appt.

---

**MONTANO'S BAKERY**
Baker's Assistant needed 6 days, 6 AM–12 noon. Apply 27 Chestnut St., Bixford. No phone calls, please.

---

**SUMMER ONLY—BUS BOYS**
at Chef's Delight. No experience necessary. Openings in Bixford and Yorktown. 5–10 PM.

---

**MOTHER'S HELPER NEEDED**
For 2 small children, Mon–Fri, 9 to 12 noon. Some light house-work. References required. Call for appointment 498-7531, between 2 and 5.

---

**GAS STATION ATTENDANT**
Gas & oil only. Prefer some experience but will train right person. 10 AM–5 PM. Good pay. Apply in person. MUTUAL OIL COMPANY, 194 Whiting St., Bix-ford.

---

**CASHIER**
Carl's Coffee Shop, 7AM–2PM, June 25 to Sept. 1 only. No expe-rience necessary. Apply in per-son, 33 Main St., Rockland.

---

1. For summer employment, many managers ask that you apply in person. Which jobs here request that you apply in person?

   _____

   _____

2. Only one of the job listings tells you the salary. Which one is it?

   _____

   _____

3. Which job listings say they will take a person with no experience?

   _____

   _____

4. Name two jobs that are mornings only.

   _____

   _____

5. Name one summer job that is evenings only.

   _____

6. Some summer jobs are part-time (about 20 hours a week). How many of these jobs are part-time? What are they?

   _____

   _____

   _____

7. Does the gas station attendant have to fix cars?

   _____

8. Will the mother's helper probably have to wash some dishes and vacuum some rugs? Answer yes or no.

   _____

---

## D A T A   B A N K

| | | | |
|---|---|---|---|
| experience | apply | train | employment |
| employer | part-time | salary | |

---

**Skill Objective: Reading and comparing "Help Wanted" ads.** Allow time for students to read the ads. Discuss any unfamiliar vocabulary and/or abbreviations. Ask students: *Which summer job sounds the most interesting? Why? What sort of work would you do? Which job has the most/fewest hours? Which job is at night?* Students may complete the page independently or working in pairs.

33

# Work Places

**Read the following paragraphs. Tell where the people work.** The first one is done for you.

1. Bill comes to work every day at 7:00. He feeds the animals their breakfast. He makes sure they are feeling well. Right now, he is teaching a monkey to do a new trick.

   Bill works _____ *in a zoo.* _____

2. Susan arrives at work at 8:00. She talks to the news director and the weather forecaster. At 12:00, her program begins. Right now, Susan is reading the news.

   Susan works _____

3. Carlos reports to work at 8:30. He looks at some loan applications. People ask him about loans and different kinds of accounts every day. Right now, Carlos is helping a customer to open a new savings account.

   Carlos works _____

4. Nancy Thomas gets to work at 7:15. Every day she erases the front chalkboard and writes a new exercise for the students to copy. Right now, she is making out a test for her third period class.

   Nancy works _____

5. Dana and Pat work from 9:00 to 5:00. They work together. Every day they answer phones, file papers, and take dictation from the boss. Right now, they are both typing important letters to other companies.

   Dana and Pat work _____

6. Dave begins work at 11:00 P.M. He works until 7:00 in the morning. Every night he stamps prices on cereal, pet food, canned goods, and soda. He arranges food neatly on the shelves. Right now, he is sweeping the floor. Dave wants everything to look good when the boss comes in.

   Dave works _____

7. Alana gets to work at 6:00 A.M. Every day she sits in a tall glass building and watches airplanes take off and land. She talks to the pilots by radio. She tells them when it is their turn to take off. Right now, she is taking a break. Her job is very difficult.

   Alana works _____

8. Lisa works part-time after school. She gets a list from the manager every afternoon. It tells her the rooms she has to clean. Lisa makes the beds and vacuums the rugs. Right now, she is polishing the woodwork in Room 106.

   Lisa works _____

9. Lorraine works from 3:00 P.M. to 11:00 P.M. Every afternoon she checks on her patients. She gives them their medicine and takes their temperature. At night she reads their charts and prepares their medication for the morning. Right now, she is talking with a patient. She is helping him to relax.

   Lorraine works _____

## D A T A  B A N K

airport  bank  hospital  hotel  office  school  supermarket  TV station  zoo

**Skill Objectives: Drawing conclusions; building vocabulary.** Assign this page for independent work. Extension Activity: Give each student the name of a work place. The students will write short paragraphs, describing a worker's job at that place. The work place should not be mentioned by name. Students will then read the paragraphs aloud, and their classmates will guess the work place. (*Factory, restaurant, movie theater, art museum, pet shop, drugstore, insurance company, sporting goods store, clothing store, hairdresser, farm, construction site.*)

# Application Forms

If you apply for a part-time job, you will probably be given an application form to fill out. Each company has its own kind of form. But the information you have to give the company is very much the same for all companies. You almost always have to give your name, address, telephone number, and Social Security number. You also have to give the names of the schools you have attended. In addition, companies want to know what other jobs you have had. Finally, they want the names of people who know you and are willing to tell about you. (Before you list such a person as a "reference," be sure to ask his or her permission to do this.)

The sample form on this page gives you a place to write down this kind of information. **Fill it out for yourself. You may want to make a copy to take with you when you apply for a job and have to fill out an application form.**

**PERSONAL DATA**

Name _____     Social Security Number _____

Address _____     How long at this address _____

_____

Telephone _____

**EDUCATION**

|  | Name and Location | Dates Attended (from–to) | Courses |
|---|---|---|---|
| Elementary School | | | |
| Junior High or Middle School | | | |
| High School | | | |

**PREVIOUS JOBS** (list latest job first)

| From-To | Name and Location of Employer | Supervisor | Position Held and Salary | Reason for Leaving |
|---|---|---|---|---|
| | | | | |
| | | | | |
| | | | | |

**REFERENCES**

|  | Name and Address | Telephone Number |
|---|---|---|
| Personal: 1. | | |
| 2. | | |
| 3. | | |
| Business: 1. | | |
| 2. | | |
| 3. | | |

**Skill Objective: Filling out an application form.** Review this application form with the students, explaining any unfamiliar terms. Discuss possible appropriate responses to *Reason for Leaving* and *Business References*. Assign the page for independent work. Provide individual help as needed.

# Social Security

Social Security is a United States Government program. It pays money to you or your family when you retire, are disabled, are very sick, or die. Social Security is paid for by a "payroll tax." Your employer takes a small part of your pay each pay period. Your employer adds an equal amount from his or her income. This money is sent to the government to help pay for Social Security. Your part is listed on your paycheck or pay slip as FICA (Federal Insurance Contributions Act, the name of the law that set up Social Security).

To get a job, you need a Social Security number. You get a Social Security number by going to the nearest Social Security office and filling out an application form. In a few weeks you will receive a card with your number on it.

You will need to take certain things with you:

- People born in the U.S. need a legal copy of a birth certificate.
- People born outside the U.S. who are now U.S. citizens can bring one of these: (1) a naturalization certificate; (2) a U.S. citizen identity card; (3) a U.S. passport; (4) a certificate of citizenship; (5) a consular report of birth.
- People born outside of the U.S. who are aliens need to bring either an Alien Registration Card (Green Card) or a U.S. Immigration Form.

**The form asks you for certain information. Be sure that you know the answers to the following questions. Write the answers here, and make a copy to take with you to the Social Security office.**

1. Your full name (the name that you will use in work or business)

   _____

2. The name that was given to you at birth. (This may be the same, or it may not be.)

   _____

3. Your birthplace _____

4. Your date of birth _____

5. Your age at your last birthday _____

6. Your mother's full name at her birth (before she was married) _____

   _____

7. Your father's full name _____

8. Your mailing address (where letters will reach you). Include the zip code.

   _____

9. Your telephone number. (Include the area code.) _____

**Skill Objectives: Learning about Social Security; answering application form questions.** Have students read the information, then ask: *Why do you need a Social Security number? Does anyone here have a number? When did you get it? When do you get money back from the Social Security system? How can you find out where the nearest Social Security office is? When you go to the office to apply for a number, what do you have to bring?* Have students complete the page independently. Provide help as needed.

36

# Let's Go!

**Read the story. Then follow the instructions below it.**

My friend Carla is always late for school! Every morning at 7:30 I stop by her house because we walk to the bus stop together, and every morning I have to wait five minutes while she finishes breakfast or combs her hair. It really drives me crazy! Her mother says it doesn't make any difference if Carla gets up at six o'clock, six-thirty, or seven, it's just impossible for her to be on time. Some mornings Carla's mother has to drive her to school because she misses the bus. Other mornings Carla and I run to the bus stop while the bus waits for us. All the kids on the bus know who we are. Most of the time I wait for Carla, but there are a few days when her mother tells me to go ahead alone. Sometimes I think I'm crazy to put up with Carla, but she's my good friend and we always go everywhere together.

**Now pretend that Carla was a friend of yours a few years ago. Write the story again, but change it from the *present tense* to the *past tense*. Use more paper if you need to.** The first sentence is done for you.

*My friend Carla was always late for school!*

_____

_____

_____

_____

_____

_____

_____

_____

_____

_____

_____

_____

_____

_____

**Skill Objective: Using the simple past tense, regular and irregular forms.** You may wish to cover this page as an oral group activity before assigning it for independent work. Students may find sentences containing several verb phrases and/or contractions difficult to convert to the past tense.

# I'm Busy, You're Busy

**A. Make sure you know the meaning of the following important words which are underlined in the story.**

| | | | |
|---|---|---|---|
| internal | breathe | destroying | blinking |
| pumps | liquid | average | growing |
| beats | filtering | message | peels |

**B. Read the story quickly to get some general ideas about it. Then read it again more slowly to answer the questions.**

## Busy, Busy, Busy

What machine works night and day without stopping? Your body! Even when you are sleeping, your body is busily working. All of the different systems of your body are in a constant state of activity, 24 hours a day.

Most of this activity is internal, and you are hardly aware of it. For example, your heart pumps about 3,000 gallons of blood each day. It beats about 100,000 times each day. You breathe about 23,000 times a day, putting your lungs to work with every breath you take. Your stomach is busy turning solid food into liquid. Your kidneys are busy cleaning and filtering over 170 quarts of different fluids that run through your body.

All through the day, your body is destroying and replacing cells in the blood. On an average day, the body destroys 250 million red blood cells. That seems like a lot, but you really don't have to worry: you have more than 20 trillion of them in your body.

Your brain is the busiest of all your body parts. No other part of the body functions without first sending a message to the brain. On an average day, the brain receives and acts on more than a million messages from different parts of the body.

Outside of the body, things are happening, too. You are constantly blinking your eyes to keep them clean. Your hair is growing—about two hundredths of an inch every day. Finally, your skin is changing. It peels off very slowly, but by the end of about three weeks, a whole layer of skin is gone. A new layer replaces it. All of this goes on very slowly and quietly; you seldom notice these changes.

Now you know why you are so tired at the end of the day! There's a lot of activity going on inside you even when there doesn't seem to be much going on at all. Make sure to get your rest each night. Your busy body needs it.

**C. Think carefully and answer the following question.**

According to the article, people breathe about 23,000 times per day. Approximately how many times per hour does a person take a breath?

a. 12,000    b. 2,000    c. 1,000    d. 24

(Go on to the next page.)

**Skill Objectives: Identifying main idea and details; building vocabulary; making a mathematical calculation.** Review the directions with the students. After the first reading, you may wish to lead a discussion about the meaning of the highlighted vocabulary words. Encourage students to check and refine their definitions by using a dictionary.

38

**D. What is the main idea of this story?**

1. The brain is the busiest part of the human body.
2. The body destroys millions of red blood cells every day.
3. The systems in your body are constantly at work, when you are awake and when you're asleep.
4. To stay healthy, always get a good night's sleep.

**E. Use a word from the underlined vocabulary to complete each of these sentences.**

1. The secretary has a _____ for her boss.

2. When ice melts, it turns from solid to _____.

3. Our new cat is too playful; he is _____ our home!

4. The baby is _____ so quickly that she can't fit into her jacket any more.

5. It's hard to look at the sun without _____.

**F. Use the story to answer these questions. Use short answers.**

1. About how many times does your heart beat each day? _____

2. About how many red blood cells does the body destroy each day? _____

3. About how many red blood cells does the average person have? _____

4. About how many messages does the brain receive each day? _____

5. About how much does the average person's hair grow each day? _____

**G. Test your knowledge of body language! Match each action with its corresponding body part by writing the letter of the body part in the blank following the action. Use the dictionary if you need to.**

1. blink or wink _____
2. nod or shake _____
3. sniff or smell _____
4. lick _____
5. grin or whistle _____
6. bite _____
7. snap or cross _____
8. crane _____
9. sprain or twist _____
10. stub _____

a. ankle
b. tongue
c. head
d. nose
e. neck
f. mouth
g. eyes
h. teeth
i. fingers
j. toe

**Skill Objectives: Recalling details; building vocabulary.** Students should complete these exercises independently. Extension Activity: Display a diagram of the organs in the human body. Have students locate the organs mentioned in this article: brain, heart, lungs, stomach, kidneys. Teach the names of other internal body parts and discuss their functions (veins, arteries, liver, intestines, etc.)

# Word Skills: Adding "-ing"

When you write verbs in the present continuous and past continuous tenses, you use the ending *-ing*. Here are some rules to help you add that ending.

**Rule 1:** For words that end in a silent (not pronounced) *e*, drop the *e* and add *ing*. Example: *smile, smiling.*

**Rule 2:** For one-syllable words that end in consonant-vowel-consonant (except *x* and *w*), double the last letter and add *ing*. Examples: *sit, sitting; run, running.*

**Rule 3:** For most other words (including words that end in *y*), add *ing* with no changes. Examples: *rain, raining; send, sending.*

**A. Now use these rules to add *-ing* to the following words:**

| | | |
|---|---|---|
| 1. shave _____ | 16. hope _____ | 31. save _____ |
| 2. comb _____ | 17. jump _____ | 32. tap _____ |
| 3. make _____ | 18. joke _____ | 33. carry _____ |
| 4. feed _____ | 19. marry _____ | 34. buy _____ |
| 5. do _____ | 20. put _____ | 35. sew _____ |
| 6. empty _____ | 21. say _____ | 36. eat _____ |
| 7. jog _____ | 22. talk _____ | 37. write _____ |
| 8. take _____ | 23. stop _____ | 38. dream _____ |
| 9. vacuum _____ | 24. type _____ | 39. cut _____ |
| 10. go _____ | 25. use _____ | 40. roar _____ |
| 11. sleep _____ | 26. worry _____ | 41. snap _____ |
| 12. wax _____ | 27. look _____ | 42. dig _____ |
| 13. change _____ | 28. bat _____ | 43. bury _____ |
| 14. fry _____ | 29. dance _____ | 44. see _____ |
| 15. get _____ | 30. hurry _____ | 45. skate _____ |

**B. Now write a sentence on another piece of paper for each of the *-ing* words you made. If you wish, you may use more than one *-ing* word in a single sentence.** For example: *While Dad was _____ing, Bob was _____ing on the telephone and I was upstairs _____ing.*

**Skill Objective: Constructing gerunds; applying rules for spelling changes.** Review the rules for spelling changes with the class. Do several examples together, then assign the page for independent work. After Part B has been completed, ask each student to read his/her favorite sentence aloud to the class.

# Thank You

When someone gives you something, you say "Thank you." Sometimes, however, a letter or note is expected. "Thank-you" notes are usually sent:

   a. when someone sends you a gift—for example, a birthday or Christmas present;

   b. when you have visited someone—for example, for a weekend or a vacation.

Here are two different kinds of "thank-you" notes:

February 8
Dear Carolina,
   The scarf you sent to me is just beautiful. It's just the color I needed to go with my gray coat, and it's so soft! Thank you so much. It was sweet of you to remember my birthday.
                     Love,
                     Lucy

May 16
Dear Anh,
   I had a wonderful time at your home last weekend. I was a little nervous at first, but everyone was so friendly I felt right at home. Thank you very much for having me.
                     Sincerely,
                     Ngoc

Notice that the notes are short and that they are written by hand, not typewritten. "Thank-you" notes should be sent promptly, within a month for gifts, and within a week after your return for visits.

**Practice writing a thank-you note. Use the space below. Write your note to an aunt who has just sent you a sweater for your birthday. Or, if you have just received a gift or come back from a visit, write a note thanking the person who gave you the gift or asked you to visit.**

**Skill Objective: Writing a thank you note.** Read and discuss the information on this page with the class. Draw attention to the opening (Dear . . .) and closing (Love, or Sincerely,) used in a friendly letter. Have students note the indention used. The date is often written in the upper right hand corner; the closing is then aligned with the date. Circulate around the room as students write their notes, offering help as needed.

41

# Dear Dot

Dear Dot—

I am very angry with my children. Six weeks ago they found a puppy and brought it home. They promised me that they were going to feed it and walk it and take care of it. It was so little and cute that I decided they could keep it, even though I don't like dogs very much. Here's my problem: no one takes care of the puppy. I walk it every day. I feed it and clean up after it. No one else can seem to find the time. Dot, I am busy, too, and I don't want to be responsible for this dog. What can I do?

Fido's Nursemaid

1. Who is angry with the children? _____

2. What did the children promise? _____

_____

3. What does Nursemaid do every day? _____

_____

4. Why doesn't anyone else take care of the dog? _____

_____

5. What does the word *promised* in this letter mean? Circle the best answer.

   a. lied        b. broke        c. stole        d. assured

6. What is your advice to Fido's Nursemaid? Discuss your answer in class. Then read Dot's answer and tell why you agree or disagree. Dot's advice is below.

Dear Nursemaid—

Remind your children about their promise to take care of the dog. After supper, keep them at the table until they complete a schedule, showing when each one is going to be responsible for the puppy. If anyone misses a day, give him or her extra chores to do around the house. Tell them that if they don't cooperate, you might have to take the dog to the pound—and remind them about what happens there.

Dot

## Write About It

**On your paper, make a list of rules or write a paragraph that explains the responsibilities of owning a pet.**

**Skill Objectives: Reading for details; drawing conclusions; understanding words through context; making judgments.** Have students read the letter and answer the questions independently. Students can write their advice to "Fido's Nursemaid" on a separate piece of paper. Correct the first five questions as a class, then have students compare and discuss their own advice and Dot's reply. You may wish to assign the "Write About It" topic as homework.

# The Present Perfect Tense (1)

The present perfect tense is used to tell about something that happened at an unspecified time in the past. To form the present perfect, use *have* or *has* with the past participle of the main verb. Look at these examples with *eat.*

| I<br>You<br>We<br>They } have eaten. | He<br>She<br>It } has eaten. |
|---|---|

Present perfect (unspecified):
I have eaten there twice.
Past (specified)
I ate there last night.

**A.** **Use *have/has* and the past participle (see Data Bank) to complete these sentences.** The first one is done for you.

1. Carlos ___*has been*___ (be) to Chicago three times.

2. Mary and Bob _____ (go) to Miami often.

3. I _____ (eat) at the restaurant twice.

4. It _____ (snow) twice so far this winter.

5. Susan _____ (read) that book before.

6. My cousins _____ (see) that movie several times.

### D A T A   B A N K

| been | eaten | gone | read | seen | snowed |
|---|---|---|---|---|---|

**B.** **Write the past participle form of the verbs below.** If the verb is regular *(-ed)* in the past form, it is also regular *(-ed)* in the past participle form. The present and past forms of each verb are given; you fill in the past participle. **Refer to pages 121 and 122 if you need to.** The first two are done for you.

1. apply/applied ___*applied*___
2. begin/began ___*begun*___
3. break/broke _____
4. bring/brought _____
5. buy/bought _____
6. call/called _____
7. choose/chose _____
8. come/came _____
9. cost/cost _____
10. decide/decided _____
11. do/did _____
12. drive/drove _____
13. enjoy/enjoy _____
14. fall/fell _____

15. find/found _____
16. get/got _____
17. give/gave _____
18. have/had _____
19. increase/increased _____
20. keep/kept _____
21. know/knew _____
22. leave/left _____
23. live/lived _____
24. lose/lost _____
25. make/made _____
26. meet/met _____
27. move/moved _____
28. pay/paid _____

**Skill Objectives: Using the present perfect tense; forming regular and irregular past participles.** Introduce/review the construction and use of the present perfect tense. Read the material at the top of the page and explain the difference between "specified" and "unspecified." *Part A:* Do the items orally together. Then assign for independent written work. *Part B:* See how many past participles students can fill in without referring to pages 121-122. Then have them use these pages to complete the others.

# The Present Perfect Tense (2)

**A.** The President of a large company has to travel to different countries on business. Here is a list of countries he has visited since 1988 when he became president.

| 1988 | 1989 | 1990 |
|---|---|---|
| February: Spain | January: Japan | February: Brazil |
| May: England | March: Mexico | April: Spain |
| June: Japan | July: Italy | May: Canada |
| September: Brazil | August: Canada | August: Japan |
| October: Mexico | November: China | December: Mexico |

**Use the information above to answer these questions. Answer in complete sentences.** The first ones are done for you.

1. How many times has the president been to _____ ?

   a. Spain _He's been to Spain twice._____

   b. Japan _____

   c. Italy _____

   d. Mexico _____

2. When did the President go to _____ ?

   a. Canada _He went to Canada in 1989 and 1990._____

   b. Italy _____

   c. Brazil _____

   d. China _____

**B.** Look at the box showing different uses of the present perfect tense.

> Affirmative: I have been to New York twice.
> Negative: I have never been to Spain.
> Question: Have you ever been to Canada?

**What about you? Answer in a complete sentence.** The first two are examples.

1. Have you ever eaten at McDonald's? _Yes, I have eaten there many times.___

2. Have you ever ridden a horse? _No, I have never ridden a horse.___

3. Have you ever used a computer? _____

4. Have you ever played polo? _____

5. Have you ever been to a wedding? _____

6. Have you ever moved? _____

**Skill Objective: Using present perfect and past tenses.** Review the construction and use of the present perfect tense. *Part A:* Have volunteers read the months and places the president visited in 1988, 1989, and 1990. Call attention to the first question. What tense is used? Why? Have students complete 1b, 1c, and 1d. Then have them look at 2a. What tense is used? Why? Have them complete Part A. *Part B:* Have volunteers read the three sentences in the box aloud. Go through the first two questions orally, then assign the others for independent written work.

44

# Have You Ever?

**A.** Interview three of your classmates to get answers for the ten questions below. Make notes of each student's responses on the chart.

| | (Name) | (Name) | (Name) |
|---|---|---|---|
| 1. Have you ever eaten dinner at midnight? When? | | | |
| 2. Have you ever met a famous person? Who? | | | |
| 3. Have you ever found money in the street? How much? | | | |
| 4. Have you ever cooked dinner for your family? What? | | | |
| 5. Have you ever been to Walt Disney World? When? | | | |
| 6. Have you ever slept until noon? How often? | | | |
| 7. Have you ever had a job? What? | | | |
| 8. Have you ever been in the hospital? When? Why? | | | |
| 9. Have you ever traveled by plane? Where? | | | |
| 10. Have you ever tried Italian food? What? | | | |

**B.** Use the results of your interviews to write a paragraph about your classmates. Use more paper if you need to. The first sentence is done for you.

*My classmates have done many interesting things.*

_____

_____

_____

_____

_____

_____

_____

**Skill Objectives: Using present perfect; interviewing; writing an informative paragraph.** Have a student interview first you, then several classmates with the first few questions. Model the correct answer structures. Show how to note the essential information on the interview chart. Point out the use of simple past vs. present perfect. Note that the second question is asked only if the first answer is *yes*. Provide as much group practice as needed, then have students form pairs and interview each other.

45

# Reading a Map

This is a map of part of the Rapid Transit lines of the Massachusetts Bay Transportation Authority (MBTA). The MBTA runs most public transportation in Boston and surrounding cities. This map shows the Rapid Transit lines in downtown Boston. Notice that there are four lines, called the Red, Green, Orange, and Blue lines. The map also shows some of the places that are near the stations on the four lines.

**A. Use the map to answer the questions under it. Use more paper if you need to. Be sure your answers are complete.** The first one is done for you.

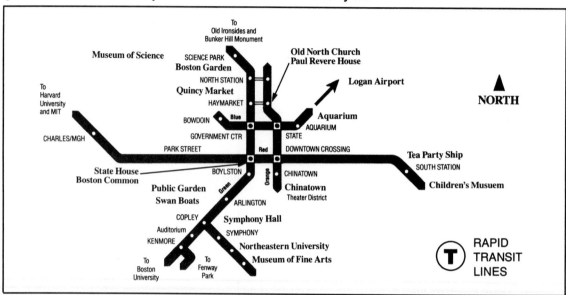

1. Using the MBTA, how can you get from Chinatown to the Aquarium?

   *Take the Orange Line north to the second stop (State). Get on the*

   *Blue Line east and take it to the first stop.*

2. How can you get from the Museum of Science to the Museum of Fine Arts?

   _____

3. How can you get from the Aquarium to Symphony Hall?

   _____

4. How can you get from the Public Garden to Chinatown?

   _____

5. How can you get from Quincy Market to Downtown Crossing?

   _____

**B. On your paper write directions to get to a "mystery stop" on the MBTA. Tell where to start, which line or lines to take, and how many stops to travel. Have a classmate read your directions and see if he or she reaches your "mystery stop."**

**Skill Objectives: Interpreting a transit map; writing and following written directions.** Read the introductory paragraph with the class. Have students trace the four lines. Call attention to the north-pointing arrowhead and review the directions north, south, east, and west. *Part A:* Work through the first question with the class and have them trace the route. Then assign the others for independent work. Correct the questions orally with the group. *Part B:* Have students work independently to write their directions. Then have them work in pairs, giving each other the directions. You may want to have several volunteers read their directions to the class.

# Water, Water Everywhere

Water is everywhere. More than three-fourths of the surface of the earth is covered by water. Everything that lives depends on water. People can get along without food for long periods, but they cannot live without water. We drink water, we swim in it, we travel on it, wash our clothes in it, and cook in it. And of course, all the fish we eat comes from the water.

Where does our water come from? Where does it go? Water is made up of two gases that we find in nature, hydrogen and oxygen. But most of the water on the earth has been here for millions of years. The water that falls as rain on your roof is the same water that fell as rain thousands of years ago. The water moves in a cycle. Let's follow a drop. As you read about the cycle, look at the picture. Use your dictionary if there are words you don't know.

1. A drop of water is on the surface of the ocean. Sunlight warms the water.
2. The drop of water evaporates and turns into water vapor—tiny droplets that float in the air.
3. The water vapor from many drops joins together to form a cloud.
4. Wind blows the cloud. When the cloud meets cold air, it turns back into drops of water and falls as rain.
5. The rain falls on land and helps plants grow. Some of it falls on mountains and flows back to the ocean as streams and rivers.
6. Some water soaks into the soil and moves underground. It comes back up to the surface through springs and wells.

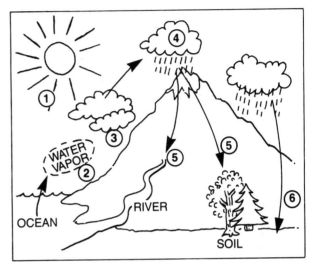

After it is used, it flows back into the soil or into rivers and then into the ocean.

**A. Look at the diagram of the water cycle below. Fill in the blanks to complete the diagram.** The numbers refer to the description of the cycle above.

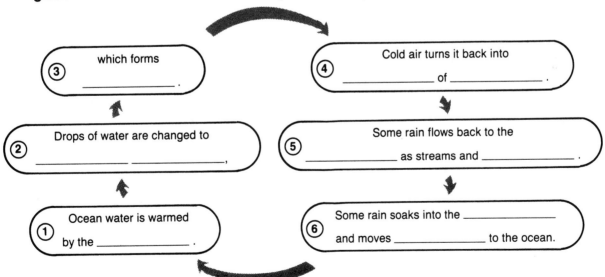

**B. On your paper, write about your feelings about water. Do you live near the ocean or a large lake? Would you like to? Why or why not? Have you had important experiences connected with water? What were they?**

**Skill Objectives: Identifying main idea and details; interpreting and completing a chart.** Have students read the story quickly to get a general idea of the subject. Ask, *What is this article about?* (topic) Have students identify unfamiliar words. Help them use context clues to discover approximate meanings. Have students reread the text, then describe the water cycle to a partner, using the diagram as a prop. Have students complete Part A independently or with a partner. Part B may be assigned as homework.

# The Declaration of Independence

**A. Make sure you know the meaning of the following important words which are under-lined in the story.**

document     equal     interfering     accusations     protected
created     preventing     simplified     forced     refused

**B. Read the story quickly to get some general ideas about it. Then read it again more slowly to answer the questions.**

## An Important Document

The Declaration of Independence is an important document in the history of the United States. Thomas Jefferson is the author of this great work. He wrote it long before he was President of the United States. The first part of the Declaration of Independence says that all men are created equal and that they have a right to life, liberty, and happiness. In the second part of the Declaration, Jefferson explained that the King of England was preventing the colonists from having these rights.

To show the world exactly how the King was interfering with the freedoms of the colonists, Thomas Jefferson included in the Declaration of Independence a long list of the King's policies in the colonies. Here is a shortened and simplified list of the accusations Thomas Jefferson made against the King of England.

1. He has taxed us against our wishes.
2. He has deprived us of our rights.
3. He has ordered British soldiers into our homes.
4. He has burned our towns.
5. He has forced Americans to serve in the British navy.
6. He has helped the Indians to attack western villages.
7. He has protected British soldiers who have murdered innocent colonists.
8. He has closed down some of our Houses of Representatives.
9. He has refused to let us have elections.
10. He has passed laws that have hurt the American people.

Thomas Jefferson ended the Declaration of Independence by saying that the thirteen colonies were no longer part of the British Empire. They did not belong to the King any more. The colonies were now the United States of America. They were a new nation in a new world.

**C. Think carefully and answer the following question.**

What did the King of England most likely think about the U.S. Declaration of Independence?

a. He agreed with it completely.
b. He liked some parts of it.
c. He was angry about it and disagreed with it.
d. He thought the colonists had some good ideas.

(Go on to the next page.)

**Skill Objectives: Reading comprehension; building vocabulary.** Review the directions with the students. After the first reading, you may want to lead a discussion about the meaning of the highlighted vocabulary words. Encourage students to check and refine their definitions by using a dictionary.

**D.** Often you can *draw a conclusion* from something you read. That is, you can figure out the answer to a question even though that answer is not stated in the reading. **Draw a conclusion to complete the following sentence. Circle your answer.**

The colonists wanted to be independent because

    a. all men are created equal.
    b. the King treated them unfairly.
    c. they wanted to be the United States of America.
    d. all men have a right to liberty and happiness.

**E. Use a word from the underlined vocabulary to complete each of the sentences.**

1. The work was too hard for the students, so the teacher _____ it.

2. The waiter cut the cake in six _____ pieces.

3. The striking workers shouted _____ in front of the factory.

4. I asked my boss for a raise but he _____ to give it to me.

5. Many politicians signed their names to this _____.

**F. Use separate paper to write answers to these questions.**

1. Who is the author of the Declaration of Independence?
2. What rights do all Americans have, according to the Declaration?
3. Who was keeping these rights from the colonists?
4. How did Thomas Jefferson end the Declaration of Independence?
5. What was the new name for the American colonies?

**G. Find details in the story that best complete the following outline.**

THE DECLARATION OF INDEPENDENCE

  A. The Introduction (The First Part)

    1. _____

    2. _____

  B. The Accusations Against the King

    1. _____

    2. _____

    3. _____

    4. _____

    5. _____

  C. The Conclusion (The Ending)

    1. _____

    2. _____

**Skill Objectives: Drawing conclusions; recalling details; building vocabulary; completing an outline.** Students should complete the exercises independently. In Part G, Section B, they may choose any five of the accusations listed against the king. Extension Activity: Looking at a map, have students guess the 13 colonies that signed the Declaration. (NH, Mass, RI, Conn, NY, NJ, Del, Pa, Md, Va, NC, SC, Ga.) Have students count the red and white stripes on the U.S. flag. Note that these stripes represent the original 13 states.

**49**

# Word Skills: Adding "-ed"

When you write the past tense and the past participle of regular verbs, you use the ending -ed. Here are some rules to help you add that ending.

**Rule 1:** For words that already end in e, simply add the letter d. Examples: *love, loved; like, liked.*

**Rule 2:** For words that end in a consonant followed by y, change the y to i and add ed. Examples: *marry, married; hurry, hurried.*

**Rule 3:** For most words that end in a vowel followed by y, simply add ed with no changes. Examples: *play, played; stay, stayed.*

**Rule 4:** For one-syllable words that end in consonant-vowel-consonant (except x), double the last letter and add ed. (NOTE: Never double final x.) Examples: *stop, stopped; jog, jogged.*

**Rule 5:** For most other words (including words that end in x), simply add ed with no changes. Examples: *wish, wished; enter, entered.*

**Rule 6:** Irregular verbs. There is no rule you can follow when you write the past participle forms of *irregular* verbs. You have to memorize them.

**A.** Now use these rules to form words in the chart below. Use pages 121–122 for help if you need to. The first two rows are completed for you.

| Present | Past | Past Participle |
|---|---|---|
| walk | *walked* | *walked* |
| go | went | gone |
|  | rode |  |
|  |  | visited |
| speak |  |  |
|  | thought |  |
| practice |  |  |
|  |  | written |
| play |  |  |
|  | built |  |
| win |  |  |
|  | spent |  |
| save |  |  |
|  | worried |  |
|  |  | married |

**B.** Now write a sentence on your own paper for each of the past or past participle words in the chart. If you wish, you may use more than one of these words in a single sentence.
For example: *She practiced her speech before she spoke to the class.*

**Skill Objectives: Forming present, past, and past participle forms; observing spelling changes.** *Part A:* Go over the six rules together. Work through the first two rows as a class. Be sure students understand why they have been completed as they have. Then assign the remaining rows as independent work. See how many each student can complete without having to consult pages 121-122, but allow them to refer to these pages to finish Part A. *Part B:* You may wish to limit the number of sentences to those where students had to fill in the second or third column. Be sure the present perfect tense is used correctly in sentences using the past participle.

50

# What Have They Done?

**Read each of the following stories. Tell what the people have done. Use the Data Bank to help you with the past participles, but answer each question in a complete sentence.** The first one is done for you.

1. Miguel is very happy as he walks into the house. He is waving a pink certificate in the air. He shouts, "I got it! I got it!" He says, "Now I can drive to work, to school, and on dates."

    What has Miguel done? *He has gotten his license.*

2. Mary opens the envelope slowly. She takes out the report card. "I don't dare look at my history grade," she says. Finally she looks. "It's a C," she says joyfully. "I won't have to go to summer school."

    What has Mary done? _____

3. Trang rereads her pages. She types the footnotes and the bibliography. "It took more than a month, but it's finished," she says to herself happily.

    What has Trang done? _____

4. Mark and Bob come late to work for the third time in a week. Mr. Carmiletti, their boss, sees them. At the end of the shift, he calls them to the office. "Boys, don't come back in tomorrow. You're fired," he tells them.

    What have the boys done? _____

5. Connie and Joanne come in from outside. "We have plenty of fresh ingredients for tonight's salad," says Joanne. "It's all from our own garden," says Connie.

    What have they done? _____

6. "No wonder we're lost," says Mrs. Ramirez, looking up from the directions. "You took Exit 23, and we were supposed to take Exit 32." "We'd better get back on the Interstate, I guess," says Mr. Ramirez.

    What has Mr. Ramirez done? _____

7. The Wilson twins are six years old and they feel very proud of themselves. Their mother was napping, and they did a chore without her asking. They put the plates, knives, forks, spoons, and napkins out for dinner.

    What have the children done? _____

8. Mr. Li looks at the clock. It is 6:15, but he doesn't have to get up this morning. He has been going to work for 40 years, but last Friday was his last day on the job. He's going to take it easy and spend more time with his family.

    What has Mr. Li done? _____

## DATA BANK

| | | |
|---|---|---|
| picked (lettuce and tomatoes) | passed (the course) | retired (from his job) |
| gotten (his license) | written (her term paper) | taken (the wrong turn) |
| lost (their jobs) | | set (the table) |

**Skill Objectives: Predicting outcomes; reviewing present perfect tense.** Explain unfamiliar words. Have students work in pairs to come up with correct answers. Be sure students write complete sentences. You may wish to make this page a contest, with the winners being the first pair to finish with correct answers.

51

## Dear Dot

Dear Dot—

My father is a grouch. When he comes home, he never says "hello" or asks how I am. Instead he says, "Have you done your homework?" or "Have you cleaned your room?" His other favorite question is "Have you emptied the trash?" His first question to my mother is, "Have you cooked dinner yet?" After dinner he isn't quite as grouchy, but he's never in a really good mood. I can't stand much more of his grouchiness. I have thought of getting my own apartment, but I am only sixteen and still in school. What can I do?

Donna

1. What questions does Donna's father ask her when he comes home? _____

_____

2. What question does he ask her mother? _____

_____

3. When is Donna's father less grouchy? _____

4. What has Donna thought of doing? _____

_____

5. What does the word *mood* in this letter mean? Circle the best answer.

   a. room        b. state of mind        c. verb        d. change of heart

6. What is your advice to Donna? Discuss your answer in class. Then take Dot's role and write your answer to Donna's letter. Tell her what to do and what not to do.

   *Dear Donna* _____ ,

   _____

   _____

   _____

   _____

   _____

   _____

   _____

                                                                  _____

**Skill Objectives: Reading for details; drawing conclusions; making judgments; writing a letter.** Have students read the letter and answer questions 1-5 independently. Correct these as a class. Then have students discuss question 6 and write their letters. Have several volunteers read their letters and have the class make suggestions for rephrasing, etc. As an additional option, ask students to write a descriptive paragraph about a happy person, telling what he or she looks like and what his or her attitude toward life is. (Student may be the subjects of their own paragraphs if they are that kind of person.)

# Can You? Could You?

**A. Answer these questions.** The first two are done for you. Use them as models.

1. Can you speak English? _____Yes, I can._____

2. Could you speak English last summer? _____No, I couldn't._____

3. Can you ride a horse? _____

4. Could you find your shoes this morning? _____

5. Can you type? _____

6. Could you tell time when you were four years old? _____

**B. Complete the sentence with *can, can't, could,* or *couldn't*.** The first one is done for you.

1. Today, in many cities, girls _____can_____ take an auto mechanics course in high school. Twenty-five years ago, girls _____ take this course in most schools.

2. If you are not an American citizen, you _____ vote for President.

3. A good runner, like Margarita, _____ run more than five miles in half an hour.

4. As a boy, Mr. Ruiz was a good football player. He _____ paly very well.

5. Pam and Sam _____ go to the beach yesterday because it was raining hard.

6. Emily Yee lives in San Francisco. On sunny days, she _____ see the Golden Gate Bridge from her window, but on foggy days she _____ .

7. If you use the yellow pages, you _____ find the number of a hospital.

8. Because Beethoven was deaf, he _____ hear the last symphonies he wrote.

9. There are lots of snow last winter, so Kevin _____ go skiing often.

10. Twenty-five years ago in most high schools, boys _____ take a cooking course, but now they _____ take one.

11. I like to listen to music, but I _____ play the piano at all.

12. Carmen is blind now, but when she was young, she _____ see very well.

**Skill Objective: Using modals *can/can't, could/couldn't*.** Teach/review the modals by asking students questions and writing on the board: *Could you walk on your hands two years ago? Can you walk on your hands now? Can you name ten states? Could you do your math homework last night?* Assign the page for independent work. Extension Activity: Have students complete these sentences any way they like: *. . . years ago, I couldn't . . ., but I can now. . . . years ago, I could . . ., but I can't now.*

53

# A True Genius

**A. Make sure you know the meaning of the following important words which are underlined in the story.**

perfected    laboratory    wires, wiring    supply    shortage
public    dynamos    sockets    substitute    genius

**B. Read the story quickly to get some general ideas about it. Then read it again more slowly to answer the questions.**

## Thomas Edison

Most people know that Thomas Edison invented the first working light bulb, but they don't know anything else about him. Edison had almost no formal schooling, he had a hearing loss most of his life, yet he invented over 1,000 different things. Among Edison's most successful inventions are: the electric vote recorder, the phonograph (record player), the dictating machine, the mimeograph (duplicator), the movie camera, and the movie projector.

Thomas Edison perfected his electric light bulb in 1879, but there was still much work to do before his invention was useful to the public. Only scientists used electricity at that time. No one knew how to use electricity safely outside of a laboratory before Thomas Edison. He and his workers had to create a safe and workable electric system.

Edison and his workers had a big job to do. First they had to build a factory. Then they had to build the dynamos (generators) to make the electricity. Next they had to put up wires to send out the electricity, and finally they had to install electric wiring and sockets in people's houses so that they could use the electricity.

Thomas Edison wanted to light up the United States electrically. To show people that he was serious, Edison began his project in New York City. It was America's largest city at that time. If Edison could bring electricity to New York, he could bring it anywhere.

By 1887, much of New York City had electricity. Edison formed the Edison Electric Light Company and continued to supply electricity to New York City and other places. His new factory, in West Orange, New Jersey, made the machines and equipment.

Thomas Edison lived until 1931. He continued to invent and perfect inventions all his life. He worked for the United States Navy in World War I. After the war, he tried to invent a substitute for rubber because of the shortage that the war caused.

Thomas Edison was a true genius, but he never went to a college or university. He was completely self-taught. The only time Edison attended school was when he was seven years old. He stayed for three months and never returned. Thomas Edison was a school dropout, yet he became one of America's most famous and most honored men.

**C. Think carefully and answer the following question.**

What happened after Edison wired New York City?

a. Other cities wanted electricity, too.
b. People who wanted electricity moved to New York.
c. Thomas Edison went out of business.
d. World War II began.

(Go on to the next page.)

**Skill Objectives: Reading comprehension; making inferences; building vocabulary.** Review the directions with the students. After the first reading, you may want to lead a discussion about the meaning of the highlighted vocabulary words. Encourage students to check and refine their definitions by using a dictionary.

**D. Draw a conclusion from the story to complete the following sentence. Circle your answer.**

To make money with his invention, Edison realized that he had to

a. bring electricity to the homes of the United States.
b. invent the light bulb.
c. invent the phonograph.
d. study at a university.

**E. Use a word from the underlined vocabulary to complete each of these sentences.**

1. Margarine is a _____ for butter.

2. Several scientists work in that _____.

3. We don't have any more paper; there is a _____ in the school.

4. James worked for five years before he _____ his invention.

5. Tommy can solve any problem; he's a _____.

**F. Use separate paper to write answers to these questions.**

1. How many different things did Thomas Edison invent?
2. What are some of Edison's major inventions?
3. What did Edison have to do after he perfected the light bulb?
4. Where did Edison start the first electric system? Why there?
5. What did Edison call his company?
6. What did Edison do during World War I?
7. Why did he try to invent a substitute for rubber?
8. How did Thomas Edison learn so much about science?
9. When did he attend school?
10. How long did he stay in school?

**G. Match the beginnings of the sentences at the left with their endings at the right. Write the letter of the correct ending in the blank after the beginning.**

1. Students had to read by candle, gas, or oil _____

2. Astronomers had to study the stars with the naked eye _____

3. Secretaries had to write notes and letters by hand _____

4. Cowboys had to reload their guns after every shot _____

5. Prospectors had to blast open mines with gunpowder _____

6. People had to walk up stairs in all buildings _____

7. People had to fasten their clothing with buttons and pins _____

a. until Whitcomb Judson invented the zipper.

b. until Alfred Nobel invented dynamite.

c. until Elisha Otis invented the elevator.

d. until Samuel Colt invented the six-shooter pistol.

e. until Johannes Kepler invented the astronomical telescope.

f. until Thomas Edison invented the light bulb.

g. until Christopher Sholes invented the typewriter.

**Skill Objectives: Reading for details; drawing conclusions; building vocabulary; determining cause and effect.** Students should complete the page independently. Extension Activity: Encourage students to research the inventor and date of the following inventions. Students should look in one or more encyclopedias, then report their findings to the class: *chewing gum, ballpoint pen, ferris wheel, frozen food, safety pin, barbed wire, roller skates, watches, saxophone, margarine.*

55

# Do You Have To?

*Write sentences about things people* **have to** *do.*

**A. Complete the following sentences by using *have to*, *has to* or *had to*.** The first one is done for you.

1. Carla ___*has to*___ study tonight.

2. My parents _____ pay a lot of bills every month.

3. You _____ take Physics I before you can take Physics II.

4. Lisa couldn't attend the meeting because she _____ visit her mother in the hospital.

5. My mother said I _____ vacuum the living room before I could go to the ball game.

6. My grandfather _____ weed his garden every week.

7. Mr. and Mrs. Ruiz _____ move to a different apartment after the fire destroyed their building.

8. Does Vuong _____ walk the dog when he gets home?

9. John's grandfather _____ wear his glasses when he reads the newspaper.

10. Did you _____ call the doctor about your problem?

11. You _____ insure the package before you mail it.

12. I _____ go to the doctor for a checkup yesterday.

**B. Excuses, Excuses! Think of three good excuses for each of the following situations. Use *had to* or *have to*.** The first one is done for you. Use it as a model.

Why didn't you do your homework?

1. ___*I had to cook dinner for my family.*___

2. _____

3. _____

Why can't you help me with the housework?

1. _____

2. _____

3. _____

Why couldn't Carla come to my party?

1. She _____

2. _____

3. _____

---

**Skill Objective: Using *have to*, *has to*, *had to*.** Ask several students questions. Write their responses on the board. *What do you have to do after school today? What did you have to do last weekend?* Then ask their classmates: *What does (Ana) have to do today? What do (Ravi and Lars) have to do? What did . . . have to do last week?* Assign Part A for independent work. Students may work on Part B in pairs. Encourage students to share their excuses with their classmates.

# Word Skills: Synonyms

Words that have the same or nearly the same meaning are called synonyms. *Leave* and *depart* are synonyms because they mean the same thing: The bus *leaves* at 3:00; the bus *departs* at 3:00. **Read each sentence. Find a synonym for the underlined word in the Data Bank at the bottom of the page and write it on the line following the sentence.** The first one is done for you.

1. The car isn't working; Felix is trying to <u>fix</u> it.          *repair*

2. Lorenzo's books are downstairs in the <u>basement</u>. _____

3. The scouts are going camping in the <u>forest</u> this weekend. _____

4. The houses on this <u>road</u> are beautiful. _____

5. Class is going to <u>start</u> in ten minutes. _____

6. The library is going to show a French <u>movie</u> this afternoon. _____

7. This shirt was very <u>cheap</u>; I got it on sale. _____

8. The teacher told the children not to act <u>silly</u>. _____

9. Bob exercises every day; he feels <u>great</u>. _____

10. My friend hasn't answered my letter; I'm <u>nervous</u> about that. _____

11. Larry was <u>sad</u> when his vacation was over. _____

12. Lucio is emptying the <u>trash</u> this week. _____

13. Please <u>close</u> the door when you leave. _____

14. Please don't <u>talk</u> to me when I am driving. _____

15. The boys have to <u>hurry</u> because they are late. _____

16. Mr. Chin was <u>angry</u> about losing his watch. _____

17. Tom's <u>home</u> is a very comfortable place to be. _____

18. Everyone in the club was <u>happy</u> to meet Professor Klein. _____

19. Chipmunks and mice are <u>little</u> animals. _____

20. New York and Los Angeles are <u>big</u> cities. _____

## D A T A   B A N K

| | | | | | | |
|---|---|---|---|---|---|---|
| begin | cellar | film | foolish | garbage | glad | house |
| inexpensive | large | mad | repair | rush | shut | small |
| speak | street | unhappy | wonderful | woods | worried | |

**Skill Objective: Identifying synonyms.** Go over the directions with the class, then complete the first few items together. Assign the page as independent work. Extension Activity: Review the definition of *antonym* (page 29). Have students create a chart listing first a synonym and then an antonym for each of the following words: *terrible, skinny, enjoy, difficult, grin, begin, yell, quick.*

57

# By Myself

**A. Complete each sentence with one of the following *reflexive pronouns*:**

myself   yourself   himself   herself   itself   ourselves   yourselves   themselves

1. I like _____.

2. The baby can dress _____.

3. The young man is painting a picture of _____.

4. We are buying _____ new coats today.

5. Lina is recording _____ on the tape recorder.

6. You students can be proud of _____.

7. The women built the houses _____.

8. It's true; I read it _____ last week.

9. No one is helping Paul; he's painting the fence _____.

10. You have to ask _____, "Is this the right thing to do?"

11. The firemen can't control the fire; it's going to burn _____ out.

12. Please help _____ to more food, Donna.

13. The girls are going to the library to find the answers _____.

14. We want the house for _____ this weekend.

15. He always looks at _____ in the mirror before he leaves home.

**B. Complete each sentence with the correct subject pronoun** (I, you, he, she, it, we, they).

1. _____ can see myself in this mirror.

2. _____ hit himself in the head.

3. _____ call ourselves bilingual.

4. _____ dresses herself in red every day.

5. _____ stopped yourself just in time.

6. _____ blame myself for losing the money.

7. _____ have to read this yourself.

8. _____ is always talking to himself.

9. _____ need the money themselves.

**Skill Objective: Reviewing subject and reflexive pronouns.** Complete the first few items as a group, then assign for independent work. Correct as a class.

# Television Tonight

Here is part of the television program for one evening in a large city area. Use the program to answer the questions. The first one is done for you.

**7:00**
☐ Bodywatch / "An Ancient Form of Care" Folk and traditional medicine; acupuncture. (CC) .............. 2
☐ NBC News (CC) ............. 4
☐ ABC News (CC) ............. 5
☐ A Current Affair ............. 6
☐ Wheel of Fortune ........ 7-12
☐ PM Magazine / Are liquid diets dangerous? .................. 10
☐ Entertainment Tonight / Mel Gibson ("Lethal Weapon 2"). In stereo. ........................ 25
☐ Nightly Business Report / Market updates and indepth economic news. .................... 36-44
☐ Cheers / Evan Drake promotes Sam to corporate executive. ..... 38
☐ Facts of Life / The girls go to war with the shop's competition. .... 56
☐ All in the Family / Archie's "other woman" asks for his help. ...... 58
☐ Star Trek / "The Trouble With Tribbles" Ravenous, furry tribles, irate officials and hostile Klingons complicate an Enterprise cargo delivery. 1:00 ...................... 64
☐ Chronicle ............... A&E
☐ Movie / "The Richest Girl in the World" (1934) Miriam Hopkins, Joel McCrea. 1:30 .............. AMC
☐ Father Murphy / The orphans send for a mail-order bride (Beverly Todd) to bring some romance into Moses' life. 1:00 ................ CBN
☐ SportsCenter ........... ESPN
☐ HeartBeat / The death of a baby she delivered devastates Cory; Eve's overweight niece visits; Paul gets together with Caroline. 1:00 ... LIFE
☐ Red Sox Digest ......... NESN
☐ Inspector Gadget ........ NICK
☐ Miami Vice / Tubbs works to save Crockett and family from falling victim to an Argentinian assassin hired by drug boss Calderone. (Part 1 of 2) 1:00 ..................... USA
**7:15**
☐ Sports Nightly .......... SPO
**7:30**
☐ New Yankee Workshop / Norm uses a lathe and router to make a candle stand. (CC) ............... 2
☐ Evening Magazine .......... 4
☐ Chronicle / Hosts: Mary Richardson and Peter Mehegan. (CC) ..... 5
☐ Love Connection ........... 6
☐ Jeopardy! ............. 7-12
☐ Entertainment Tonight / Mel Gibson ("Lethal Weapon 2"). In stereo. ........................ 10
☐ A Current Affair ............ 25
☐ Newhart / Dick roasts Man-of-the-Year George at a lodge banquet. .. 38
☐ MacNeil/Lehrer NewsHour ... 44
☐ Night Court / Quon Le wants to be a citizen before she gives birth. .. 56

☐ Movie / "The Bell Jar" (1979) Marilyn Hassett, Julie Harris. 2:30 58
☐ World of Survival / Red deer romp in the Scottish Highlands. ..... A&E
☐ SpeedWeek ........... ESPN
☐ Wimbledon '89 Highlights .. HBO
☐ Crook & Chase in stereo. .. NASH
☐ Baseball / Milwaukee Brewers at Boston Red Sox. (Live) ...... NESN
☐ Looney Tunes .......... NICK
☐ Horse Racing / "Rockingham Report". ................... SPO
☐ Kate & Allie (CC) ....... WWOR
**8:00**
☐ This Old House / Exterior painting; plastering; a security system. (CC) ...................... 2
☐ The Cosby Show / Cliff meets a pregnant patient's free-spirited grandfather (Sammy Davis Jr.). In stereo. (CC) ...................... 4-10
☐ Baseball / Cincinnati Reds at New York Mets. (Live) ............ 5-12
☐ 48 Hours / Americans struggle to sober up as the effects of alcoholism become apparent. 1:00 (CC) .... 6-7
☐ Movie / "52 Pick-Up" (1986) Roy Scheider, Ann-Margaret. 2:00 ... 25
☐ Movie / "Act of the Heart" (1970) Genevieve Bujold, Donald Sutherland. 2:00 ...................... 27
☐ Are You Being Served? / The staff is trained in fire procedures. ..... 36
☐ Movie / "Dragnet" (1954) Jack Webb, Ben Alexander. 2:00 ..... 38
☐ Movie / "Psycho II" (1983) Anthony Perkins, Vera Miles. 2:00 56
☐ World Monitor / American business in China. ................ 68
☐ Durrell in Russia / Gerald and Lee Durrell examine wildlife of the Soviet Union, starting with a visit to the Moscow Zoo. ................... A&E
☐ Movie / "Return to Waterloo" (1985) Ken Colley, Valerie Holliman. 1:00 ..................... BRAVO
☐ Movie / "Johnny Holiday" (1949) William Bendix, Allen Martin Jr. 2:00 ...................... CBN
☐ Walt Disney Presents / "A Disney Vacation." ................. DIS
☐ Auto Racing / "Corvette Challenge Series" From Detroit. ........ ESPN
☐ Movie / "The Great Outdoors" (1988) Dan Aykroyd, John Candy. 1:30 ..................... HBO
☐ Spenser: For Hire / A crazed ex-convict and two cohorts try to rob a post office and end up taking hostages, including Susan and Hawk. 1:00 ..................... LIFE
☐ Movie / "The Don is Dead" (1973) Anthony Quinn, Frederic Forrest. 2:00 ..................... MAX
☐ Nashville Now / Ricky Van Shelton; Shenandoah; Shelby Lynne. In stereo. .................... NASH

☐ Mr. Ed / Ed wants to be a one-horse band in Carol's variety show. ...................... NICK
☐ Camp Meeting, U.S.A. ..... PTL
☐ Baseball / United States vs. Taiwan. From Tulsa, Okla. (Live) ... SPO
☐ Movie / "The Barbarians" (1987) David Paul, Peter Paul. 1:30 ... TMC
☐ Movie / "They Were Expendable" (Color) (1945) Robert Montgomery, John Wayne. 2:55 ........... TNT
☐ Murder, She Wrote / Jessica seeks the killer of an arrogant professor (George Grizzard) with many enemies. Guest: Shaun Cassidy. 1:00 .... USA
☐ Bonanza / Newspaperman Samuel Clemens (Howard Duff), writing as Mark Twain, heads a fight against a judge involved in land fraud. 1:00 ................... WWOR

**Cable Key**

| | |
|---|---|
| A&E — Arts and Entertainment | NASH — Nashville |
| BRAVO — Bravo Network | NESN — N.E. Sports Network |
| CBN — Cable Network | SPO — Sports Network |
| DIS — Disney | SHO — Showtime |
| ESPN — Entertainment/Sports Network | TMC — The Movie Channel |
| HBO — Home Box Office | USA — USA Network |
| LIFE — Lifetime | WWOR — New York |
| MAX — Cinemax | WTBS — Atlanta |

1. The schedule gives programs starting at _7:00 p.m._ .

2. People with hearing problems can watch close captioned news on channels _____ and _____ at _____ P.M.

3. How many movies are being shown at 8:00 tonight? _____

4. The program I'd like to watch at 8:00 is _____ because _____ .

5. There are _____ cable TV programs starting at 7:30.

6. "DIS" on cable means _____ .

7. Three sports channels on cable are _____ , _____ , and _____ .

8. The sports you can watch tonight are _____ and _____ .

9. You can see a program about alcoholism at _____ .

10. The movie with John Wayne is _____ _____ .

CC = closed captioned for people with hearing problems

**Skill Objective: Reading a TV schedule.** Have students skim the TV schedule. Point out that it is from an area that has cable television as well as broadcast TV. Ask various students, *What show would you watch at 8:00? What channel is it on? When is the show over?* Assign the page for independent work. As an extension, ask students to get a TV schedule for the coming week, and each day, circle the shows they watch. At the end of the week, have students graph the number of hours they watched TV each day. Bar or line graphs can be used.

# How Does It Work?

What really happens when you press a button or turn a dial on your electric stove? How does an electric stove work?

Inside and on top of an electric stove there are thick wires called heating elements. Often they are covered with metal to protect them. When you turn the stove on, electricity moves through the heating element, and the element becomes red hot.

The element gets hot because the wire resists the flow of the electric current. When you rub your hands together, each hand resists the movement of the other, and they get hot. In the same way, the heating element gets hot from resisting the current forcing its way through it.

The heat from the element goes into the food in the oven or on top of the stove. After you give the food the right amount of heat, it is ready.

If you don't have an electric stove, you can see this same process by looking at a toaster or toaster oven. The basic principle of electric cooking is the "resistance wire" called the heating element.

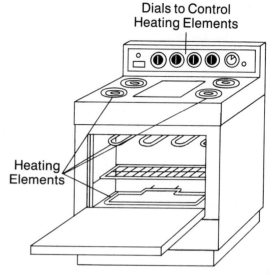

Dials to Control Heating Elements

Heating Elements

## A. Read the article and answer the questions.

1. According to the article, what causes food to cook in an electric stove? Circle your answer.

   a. electricity running through the food

   b. electricity running through the button or dial

   c. electricity running through the heating element

2. What causes the heating element to get hot?

   a. electricity runs through it very easily

   b. it has great resistance to electricity

   c. it is covered with metal

3. Use the numbers 1 through 5 to show the sequence in which things happen when you cook food on an electric stove.

   _____ The heating element gets hot.

   _____ The food is ready.

   _____ Electricity flows through the heating element.

   _____ You press the button or turn the dial.

   _____ The food absorbs the heat.

## B. A gas stove works very differently from an electric stove. Find out how a gas stove works and write a short composition about it on your own paper.

**Skill Objectives: Determining cause and effect; sequencing.** Have students read the article silently. Tell them to look at the diagram as each part is mentioned. They may want to reread one or more times to be sure they understand how the stove works. *Part A:* Tell students they are going to scan, or look quickly through the article to find specific information that will help them answer the questions. *Part B:* Students can find information about gas stoves in books or encyclopedias. The school librarian can help them locate this information.

## Dear Dot

Dear Dot—

We are going to have to move soon, and my husband and I are having trouble deciding where to go. I want to stay in the city. Fred wants to buy a house way out in the suburbs. He works at home, so he isn't going to have to commute. But I am going to have to drive 35 miles to work every day. I am going to have to get up earlier, and arrive home later each evening. Besides, I love the city and I hate to drive! Dot, we don't know what to do. How can we compromise?

City Lover

1. What are City Lover and her husband going to have to do soon? _____

_____

2. What does her husband want to do? _____

_____

3. Why does City Lover not want to do what her husband wants? _____

_____

_____

4. What does the word *commute* in this letter mean? Circle your answer.

   a. speak with someone    b. add up    c. arrange something    d. drive to and from a place

5. What is your advice to City Lover? Discuss your answer in class. Then write a letter to her telling her what you think she should do.

*Dear City Lover* _____ ,

_____

_____

_____

_____

_____

_____

                                                                        _____

**Skill Objectives: Reading for details; drawing conclusions; making judgments; writing a letter.** Have students read the letter and answer questions 1-4 independently. Correct these as a class. Then have students discuss question 5 and write their letters. Have several volunteers read their letters and have the class make suggestions for rephrasing, etc. As an additional option, ask students to write a paragraph about where they would like to live (city, country, suburbs), listing the advantages of the area they choose.

61

# The Party

**A. As you read the story to yourself, change the verbs in parentheses to the past tense. Then write the whole story with the past tense verbs. Use more paper if you need to.**

I am so embarrassed! Here's my story. Last week my girlfriend Astrid (invite) me to a party at her house. She (tell) me that all our friends (are) coming, and also the new boy who just (move) in across the street. I (am) excited about the party, and I (want) to make a good impression. I (go) to Lord and Taylor and (buy) a new pair of slacks and a beautiful new blouse. I also (find) a nice pair of shoes. I (decide) to go to the hairdresser, too. I (spend) a lot of money. When I (get) home from the hairdresser's, I (take) a bath and (put) on my new clothes. I (think) I (look) great! I (feel) happy and excited about the party.

At eight-thirty, I (walk) over to Astrid's house and (ring) the doorbell. Astrid (answer) and (say), "Oh, hi, Luisa. What are you doing here?" I (say) "The party's tonight, isn't it?" She (say), "Oh, no! The party isn't tonight, it's tomorrow night!"

I (feel) so stupid. I (go) to the party on the wrong night!

_____

_____

_____

_____

_____

_____

_____

_____

_____

**B. Now read each of the sentences below. Write _T_ if the sentence is true. Write _F_ if it is false. Write _?_ is the story doesn't give you enough information to decide.**

_____ 1. Astrid is the person who was giving the party.

_____ 2. Luisa is the person who went to the party on the wrong night.

_____ 3. The party was on a Saturday night.

_____ 4. Luisa bought a new dress for the party.

_____ 5. Luisa wanted to impress the new neighbor across the street.

_____ 6. Luisa paid a lot of money for her new clothes.

_____ 7. When Astrid answered the door, she probably looked puzzled.

_____ 8. Luisa was embarrassed because she was too late for the party.

_____ 9. Astrid probably forgot to ask when the party was.

**C. On your paper, write about an embarrassing experience you have had. Tell what happened, when and where it happened, and how you felt about it.**

**Skill Objectives: Simple past, regular and irregular forms; reading for details; writing an autobiographical paragraph.** Have volunteers read some sentences aloud, changing the verbs to the past tense. Cover some or all of the paragraph in this manner before assigning the page for independent work. Students may refer to the lists on pages 121 and 122 to check the spelling of regular and irregular past tense verbs. Part C may be used as a homework assignment.

# Persons and Places

**A. Read each sentence. Use the Data Bank to find the person it describes.** The first one is done for you.

1. He's a person who helps you plan a vacation or trip.     *travel agent*

2. She's a person who writes books, plays, or stories.     _____

3. He's a person who cuts meat at the supermarket.     _____

4. She's a person who fills cavities and pulls teeth.     _____

5. He's a person who stays with young children when their parents go out for the evening.     _____

6. She's a person who gives you information when you dial 411 or 1-555-1212.     _____

7. He's a person who decides if a baseball player is out or is safe.     _____

8. She's a person who leads a chorus or an orchestra.     _____

**B. Use the Data Bank to find the place each sentence describes.** The first one is done for you.

1. It's a place where there is lots of sand and very little rain.     *desert*

2. It's a place where people play basketball.     _____

3. It's a place where you go to wash your clothes.     _____

4. It's a place where you go when you want to shop in many different kinds of stores.     _____

5. It's a place where you go to see clowns, animals, and acrobats.     _____

6. It's a place where you go to see famous paintings and drawings.     _____

7. It's a place where you go to buy a watch or a necklace.     _____

8. It's a place where you go to buy a sofa or a bed.     _____

## D A T A  B A N K

| | | | | | |
|---|---|---|---|---|---|
| author | babysitter | butcher | circus | conductor | court |
| dentist | desert | furniture store | jewelry store | laundromat | mall |
| museum | operator | travel agent | umpire | | |

**C. Finish these sentences. Use *who* or *where* in each sentence.** The first one is done for you.

1. An astronaut *is a person who travels in space.* _____

2. A lawyer _____

3. A stadium _____

4. A zoo _____

5. An architect _____

**Skill Objectives: Using adjective clauses with *who* and *where*; discussing occupations and community places; drawing conclusions.** Have students complete Parts A and B independently. Draw attention to the phrases "a person who" and "a place where." Have students complete Part C. Ask volunteers to read their favorite sentence aloud. Extension Activity: Some students may enjoy creating crossword puzzles with occupation and community places vocabulary. Check the puzzles for accuracy, then reproduce and distribute to the class to solve.

63

# A Nation of Immigrants (1)

**A.** Look at the two graphs on this page. They show the number of people who immigrated (came into) the United States in each ten-year period from 1821 to 1980. They also show where these people came from. Use the graphs to complete the sentences. The first one is done for you.

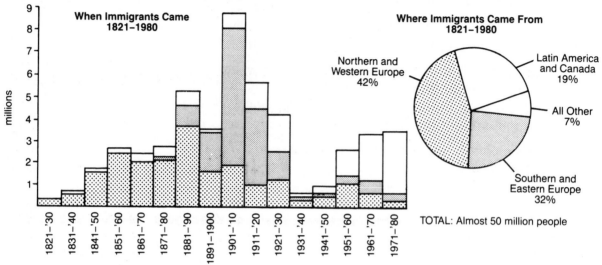

**When Immigrants Came 1821–1980**

**Where Immigrants Came From 1821–1980**

Northern and Western Europe 42%

Latin America and Canada 19%

All Other 7%

Southern and Eastern Europe 32%

TOTAL: Almost 50 million people

1. Almost __*50*__ million people came to the United States between 1820 and 1980.

2. Most of the people who first came were from _____ .

3. Most of those who came between 1950 and 1980 were from _____ .

4. People from Southern and Eastern Europe were the largest number of immigrants in

   the period from _____ to _____ .

5. About _____ million people came from Northern and Western Europe between 1821 and 1980.

6. About _____ million immigrants came to the United States between 1901 and 1910.

7. About _____ million immigrants have come from Latin America and Canada since 1821.

8. People from _____ started coming around 1870.

9. Not many immigrants came between 1930 and 1940 probably because _____

   _____ (Hint: look at page 14.)

10. The round graph is called a "pie chart" because _____

    _____

**B.** The United States has been called "a nation of immigrants." On your paper, write a paragraph telling why this is or is not a good name. Are there any people in the United States who are not immigrants or descendants of immigrants? Discuss your answer with others in the class.

---

**Skill Objectives: Interpreting graphs; writing a paragraph.** Read the introductory paragraph, then draw attention to the pie graph. Ask, *Where have most U.S. immigrants come from? Where did your family come from? How many U.S. immigrants have come from that part of the world?* Examine the bar graph. Note the shading for the immigrants' homeland is the same in both graphs. Ask, *How many immigrants came from . . . between (1911 and 1920)? Between (1861 and 1870), where did most immigrants come from?* Assign the page for independent work.

# A Nation of Immigrants (2)

On the preceding page are graphs showing the history of immigration into the United States. On this page are tables dealing with immigration for the seven-year period, 1981 to 1987. **Look at these tables. Then do Parts A and B below.**

**Table 1. Where Immigrants Were Born**

| Place | Number | Place | Number |
|---|---|---|---|
| West Indies[1] | 576,100 | Dominican Republic | 155,700 |
| Mexico | 474,100 | Jamaica | 143,200 |
| Philippines | 323,900 | Cuba | 120,900 |
| Vietnam | 289,000 | Laos | 112,000 |
| China and Taiwan | 257,100 | United Kingdom[2] | 98,900 |
| Korea | 237,600 | Cambodia | 96,100 |
| India | 173,600 | Iran | 93,400 |

**Table 2. Percents by Region**

| Region | Percent |
|---|---|
| Asia | 47.3% |
| Latin America | 38.7% |
| Europe | 10.9% |
| Canada | 1.9% |
| Other | 1.2% |

[1] Without Barbados, Cuba, Dominican Republic, Haiti, Jamaica, Trinidad and Tobago
[2] England, Scotland, Wales, Northern Ireland   Source: *Statistical Abstract of the United States,* 1989

**A. Answer these questions. Use the encyclopedia if you need to.** The first one is started for you.

1. What are three countries on Table 1 in which the people speak Spanish? _Mexico,_ _____

2. What are two countries on Table 1 in which the people speak English? _____

3. What are three Asian countries on the table? _____

4. What is one European country on the table? _____

**B. Read each of the following statements. Use the tables and your answers on Part A to decide whether it is true or false. Write *T* if it is true. Write *F* if it is false. Write *?* if the material doesn't give you enough information to decide.**

_____ 1. Most of the people who came to the U.S. between 1981 and 1987 spoke Spanish.

_____ 2. Between 1981 and 1987, the number of Cubans who came was about half the number of Koreans.

_____ 3. More people came from India than from Korea.

_____ 4. 43,000 Haitians came to the U.S. during this period.

_____ 5. The second largest group to come during this period was from the United Kingdom.

_____ 6. More people came from Canada, Europe, and Latin America combined than from Asia.

_____ 7. "Other" includes Australia, Tasmania, and New Zealand.

**C. On your paper, make graphs of the information on Tables 1 and 2.**

**Skill Objectives: Reading tables; using an encyclopedia; graphing statistics.** Help students locate the countries and regions on a world map. Students can work in pairs on Parts A and B. *Part C:* Have students draw circles and label their graphs (U.S. Immigration, 1971-1979). Using fractions will help to make accurate graphs. (48.9% = 1/2, 16.7% = 1/6, 12.3% = 1/8) Color and label each section. For the bar graph, number the vertical axis from 0-560,000 in steps of 20,000.

# What Did You See?

**A. Read the pairs of sentences. Make each pair of sentences into one sentence. Look at the example, and use it as a model for your answers.**

Example: Yesterday I saw a man. He was sleeping in the subway station.

*Yesterday I saw a man who was sleeping in the subway station.*

1. Yesterday I saw a girl. She was walking six dogs at one time!

2. Yesterday I saw an old woman. She was looking in trash cans for food.

3. Yesterday I saw a man. He was wearing a clown costume and handing out papers about the circus.

4. Yesterday I saw a boy. He was roller skating down a busy street.

5. Yesterday I saw a girl. She was eating three ice cream cones at the same time.

6. Yesterday I saw a young man on the subway. He was taking a box of kittens to the pet store.

**B. Now use the pictures to write the third line of the dialogue.** The first one is done for you.

1. —Do you know Rita Marini?

   —No, I don't. Who is she?

   *She's the girl who lives next door to me.*

2. —Do you know Kinchee Chow?

   —No, I don't. Who is she?

Skill Objective: Combining sentences with *who*. Go over the directions with the class, then assign the page as independent work.

# Word Skills: Prefixes

A prefix is a syllable or group of syllables that comes at the beginning of a word and has a special meaning. You can add a prefix to another word or root word to change the meaning of the original word or to create a new word. **Look at the list of common prefixes below and the examples of each one.**

| Prefix and Meaning | | Example and Definition | |
|---|---|---|---|
| mono | = one | monorail | train running on <u>one</u> rail |
| bi | = two | bicycle | <u>two</u>-wheeled vehicle |
| tri | = three | triangle | <u>three</u>-sided figure |
| poly | = many | polytheism | belief in <u>many</u> gods |
| un | = not | unwelcome | <u>not</u> welcome or wanted |
| pre | = before | prehistoric | <u>before</u> recorded history |
| ex | = out | export | send <u>out</u> of a country |
| sub | = under | subterranean | <u>under</u> the ground |
| inter | = between | international | <u>between</u> nations |
| re | = again | reread | read <u>again</u> |

**Now match the columns. Write the letter of the correct definition in the space next to the word. Use your dictionary if you need to.** The first one is done for you.

_b_ 1. premature

_____ 2. monotone

_____ 3. bilingual

_____ 4. exhale

_____ 5. subtitle

_____ 6. interstellar

_____ 7. polygon

_____ 8. tripod

_____ 9. unprepared

_____ 10. reorder

_____ 11. preface

_____ 12. monopoly

_____ 13. extract

_____ 14. biweekly

_____ 15. subway

_____ 16. triple

_____ 17. polygamy

_____ 18. interfere

_____ 19. rewrite

_____ 20. uncertain

a. speaks two languages

b. before the expected time

c. copy or write again

d. one company in control of an entire business

e. to remove or pull out

f. not ready

g. multiply by three

h. many-sided figure

i. translation on a foreign film

j. one constant tone of voice

k. come between

l. not sure

m. train that travels under the ground

n. breathe out

o. between the stars

p. ask for supplies again

q. every two weeks

r. three-legged support

s. introduction to a book, foreword

t. many wives for one husband

**Skill Objective: Understanding prefixes.** Go over the introduction and chart with the class. Complete the first items together. Have students identify the prefix used, recall its meaning from the chart, put it together with the root word meaning, if possible, and choose the most likely answer. Remind students to first answer the easier items, then return to the more difficult ones. Extension Activity: Have students use the twenty words in original sentences. They may use dictionaries to confirm and refine their understanding of the words.

**67**

# The Iron Horse

**A. Make sure you know the meaning of the following important words which are underlined in the story.**

| steam | iron | race | publicity | catch up |
|-------|------|------|-----------|----------|
| coal | owned | bet | accept | extended |

**B. Read the story quickly to get some general ideas about it. Then read it again more slowly to answer the questions.**

## The First Railroads

In the early days of the railroads, horses pulled the trains. The trains had no engines and no power of their own. Richard Trevithik of England invented a steam-powered engine in 1804. He used the engine to pull open cars full of coal. Soon people were building railroads and steam engines all over the world. Because the steam engines did the work that animals used to do, people called them iron horses.

Peter Cooper was a rich American businessman. He owned a lot of land near one of the new American railroads, the Baltimore and Ohio Railroad. He wanted the B&O railroad to be successful. He built his own steam engine to drive along the railroad. The train that Cooper built was very small. It was almost like a toy. Cooper called the train Tom Thumb after the storybook character who was only as big as a thumb.

Most people traveled in stagecoaches drawn by horses. A stagecoach line challenged Peter Cooper to a race. The owner of the line bet his horse could go faster than the train. Cooper agreed to the race. He wanted to get publicity for the new steam engine. He wanted people to accept the railroad.

The day of the race came. At first the horse was winning the race. The horse was able to begin the race at top speed. Tom Thumb needed time to build up steam. Peter Cooper worked hard to make the train go faster. Soon he was catching up to the horse. Finally, he caught up to the horse. After a while he went in front of the horse. Tom Thumb and Peter Cooper were going to win the race! Suddenly one of the parts of the engine broke. The train stopped. The horse rushed ahead. Peter Cooper and Tom Thumb lost the race.

Of course, that is not the end of the story. Other inventors built large and fast trains to replace Tom Thumb. Soon horses couldn't compete with the new trains. By 1870, railroads extended all across the United States. The "iron horse" had become an important part of American life.

**C. Think carefully and answer the following question.**

People accepted trains in place of horses because

a. they didn't like horses any more.
b. trains were faster than horses over long distances.
c. Peter Cooper told them to.
d. railroads pulled coal in coal mines.

(Go on to the next page.)

**Skill Objectives: Reading comprehension; drawing conclusions; building vocabulary.** Review the directions with the students. After the first reading, you may want to lead a discussion about the meaning of the highlighted vocabulary words. Encourage students to check and refine their definitions by using a dictionary.

**D. Use a word or phrase from the underlined vocabulary to complete each of these sentences.**

1. Advertising is a form of _____.

2. The gambler _____ all his money on one card game.

3. My brother left ten minutes ago; I hope I can _____ with him.

4. Some _____ is burned to make electricity.

5. A marathon is a 26-mile _____.

**E. Use separate paper to write answers to these questions.**

1. In what year did Richard Trevithik invent the railroad steam engine?
2. What did people call the new trains?
3. Why did they use this name?
4. What did Peter Cooper want?
5. What did *Tom Thumb* look like?
6. What was *Tom Thumb* racing against?
7. Why didn't *Tom Thumb* go fast right away?
8. Why did Peter Cooper lose the race?
9. What replaced *Tom Thumb*?
10. By 1870, how far did railroads extend?

**F.** Americans have always made up names for widely used inventions. Some of these names are in the column at the left. See if you can match them up with the inventions they name. **Write the letter for the invention in the blank in front of the "folk" name for it.**

_____ 1. talking machine     a. television

_____ 2. flying machine     b. aircraft carrier

_____ 3. talkies     c. electric voice amplifier

_____ 4. tin lizzie     d. coin operated phonograph

_____ 5. boob tube     e. record player

_____ 6. nickelodeon     f. tall building

_____ 7. bullhorn     g. movies with sound

_____ 8. skyscraper     h. helicopter

_____ 9. flattop     i. Ford car

_____ 10. whirlybird     j. airplane

**G.** Imagine it is 1804. People are arguing about whether trains have a future, or if America should stick with horses. **Write three arguments for each side.**

| Advantages of a Horse | Advantages of Trains |
| --- | --- |
| 1. | 1. |
| 2. | 2. |
| 3. | 3. |

## Dear Dot

Dear Dot—

My friend Larry asked me to lend him one of my records last week. I am very careful with my records, and I don't usually let people borrow them, but Larry is my best friend, so I let him take it. He returned it yesterday, and it's ruined! There are big scratches on both sides. When I bought this record last year, it cost me $8.00. Now it's even more expensive. I think Larry owes me a new record. What do you think?

Bob

1. What did Larry ask Bob last week? _____

_____

2. Why did Bob agree to do this? _____

_____

3. What is the condition of Bob's record now? _____

_____

4. What does Bob want? _____

5. What does the word *lend* in this letter mean? Circle the best answer.

   a. give for a while     b. take for a while     c. spend     d. break or ruin

6. What do you think Bob should do? Discuss your answer in class. Then write your advice in a letter to Bob. How can he get what he wants without losing a friend?

   *Dear Bob* _____ ,

   _____

   _____

   _____

   _____

   _____

   _____

   _____

   _____

**Skill Objectives: Reading for details; drawing conclusions; making judgments; writing a letter.** Have students read the letter and answer questions 1–5 independently. Correct these as a class. Then have students discuss question 6 and write their letters. Have several volunteers read their letters and have the class make suggestions for rephrasing, etc. As an additional option, have students write about a hobby or other interest, explaining what the hobby or interest is and how, where, and when they first found out about it.

# A Trip to the Moon: 1865

**Use words from the Data Bank to fill the blanks in the story. Write only one word in each blank. The same word can be used more than once, however.** The first one is done for you.

Jules Verne is a famous French author who dreamed about wonderful

machines and fantastic journeys. In 1865, Verne wrote

_____a_____ book about a trip to _____ moon. The

name of the _____ was *From the Earth to the Moon.* The

spaceship he described _____ very interesting. There were

three "astronauts" in the spaceship, two Americans and

_____ Frenchman. The _____ kept chickens

in the ship for food! _____ beds they used were very com-

fortable, _____ they cooked their meals on

_____ gas stove!

The men reached the _____ in 97 hours, 13 minutes

_____ 20 seconds after _____ had left the

earth. When they landed on the _____, they made a mis-

take and couldn't leave _____ spaceship. That was a good

thing _____ they didn't have any spacesuits!

Verne's books were very popular. _____ at that time

_____ fascinated with scientific developments and Verne

included many scientific facts. Today we call _____ like this

"science fiction."

In 1865, _____ thought Verne's dreams

_____ impossible. But one hundred years later,

_____ were walking on the moon.

## DATA BANK

| | | | | | | |
|---|---|---|---|---|---|---|
| a | and | because | book | books | men | moon |
| one | people | the | they | was | were | |

**Skill Objective: Completing a cloze exercise.** Assign this page for independent work. Correct as a class and ask comprehension questions about the story. Extension Activities: Have students check the card catalog in the school library for books by or about Jules Verne. Other students can use the encyclopedia to research Jules Verne. Have students report their findings to the class.

71

# A Trip to the Moon: 1969

Read about the first real trip to the moon by human beings.

**Read the story. Use your dictionary for any words you are not sure of.**

Have you been to the moon lately? This is a question your grandchildren might ask their friends. One hundred years ago, a trip to the moon was only a dream. One hundred years from now, a trip to the moon might be as common as a trip to the next state.

On July 20, 1969, the dream to land on the moon became a reality. Astronaut Neil Armstrong stepped out of the Apollo 11 spacecraft's lunar module and walked on the moon's rocky surface for 18 minutes. A television camera on the module permitted people from all over the earth to see a human's first step on the moon. Everyone heard Armstrong say, "That's one small step for man, one giant leap for mankind."

Astronaut Edwin Aldrin joined Armstrong for another 2½ hours. A third astronaut, Michael Collins, stayed in the spacecraft. Armstrong and Aldrin collected rocks and soil samples and set up instruments to record vibrations caused by moonquakes. They also placed an American flag on the moon. Then their lunar module took them back to the orbiting spacecraft, and they returned to earth at the speed of 25,000 miles an hour.

The three astronauts couldn't eat regular food; they had to eat dehydrated (dried) food which didn't need refrigeration. And there were no gas stoves or comfortable beds on the Apollo 11 spacecraft as there were on the imaginary spaceship described by Jules Verne. But this was not science fiction. This was the real thing! It was indeed, "one giant leap" for the human race.

**Read each sentence below and decide if it is true or false. Write _T_ if it is true. Write _F_ if it is false. Write _?_ if the story doesn't give you enough information to decide.**

_____ 1. One hundred years ago, people first traveled to the moon.

_____ 2. The first person to walk on the moon was Edwin Aldrin.

_____ 3. The astronauts walked on the moon for about three hours.

_____ 4. It took the astronauts two days to return to earth.

_____ 5. The astronauts brought back a moonquake to earth.

_____ 6. Three astronauts walked on the moon.

_____ 7. The spacecraft was the Apollo 11.

_____ 8. The astronauts ate cereal, nuts and fruit.

**Skill Objectives: Reading for details; reviewing verb tenses.** Have students read the selection quickly to get a general idea of the subject. List and discuss unfamiliar vocabulary. Students should use context clues and try to guess the meaning. Have students read the selection again and answer the questions. Extension Activities: Ask students to: a) name the main idea of the story, 2) find diagrams and photos of Apollo 11 and the lunar voyage in the library, 3) list three things people might be able to do 100 years from now.

# Space Exploration

The words *already* and *yet* are often used with the present perfect tense. Look at the box to see how they are used. The box also has a review of the present perfect and past tenses.

| | | |
|---|---|---|
| ALREADY: | Astronauts have already been to the moon. | (affirmative) |
| YET: | Astronauts haven't been to Mars yet. | (negative) |
| | Have astronauts been to Mars yet? | (question) |
| Non-specific time: | They have already been to the moon. | (present perfect) |
| Specific time: | They went there in 1969. | (past) |

**Use *already* and *yet* in the following sentences.** The first two are done for you.

1. Astronauts (be) to the moon. (affirmative)
   *Astronauts have already been to the moon.*

2. Astronauts (travel) to the planet Mars. (negative)
   *Astronauts haven't traveled to Mars yet.*

3. Astronauts (bring) back rocks from the moon. (question)
   _____

4. We (travel) to other planets. (negative)
   _____

5. Women (travel) in outer space. (affirmative)
   _____

6. We (establish) the first "city" in space. (question)
   _____

7. Astronauts (walk) and (drive) on the moon. (affirmative)
   _____

8. Astronauts (live) in a space station. (question)
   _____

9. Countries (send) communication satellites into space. (affirmative)
   _____

10. Other countries (go) to the moon. (negative)
    _____

## DATA BANK

### Past Participles

| walked | lived | gone | traveled | brought | established | been | sent |
|--------|-------|------|----------|---------|-------------|------|------|

**Skill Objective: Using the present perfect with *already* and yet.** Review the construction of the present perfect tense and remind students of the difference between non-specific and specific time, as shown in the box at the top of the page. Provide other examples on the board if necessary. If students need more practice than the two items already done for them, go through the entire page orally before assigning it for independent written work.

73

# Present Perfect *vs.* Past

The present perfect tells about something that happened at an unspecified time (or times) in the past.

I *have been* to New York three times.
He *has* already *visited* the Museum of Science.

The past tense tells about something that happened at a specific time (or times) in the past:

I *was* in New York three years ago.
He *visited* the Museum of Science last month.

**A. Read the sentences carefully and choose either the present perfect or the past form of the verb.** The first one is done for you.

1. Astronauts ___*have traveled*___ (travel) to the moon several times.

2. The first one _____ (walk) on the moon in 1969. Two years later, two Americans _____ (return) and _____ (drive) a Moon Rover. The top speed of the "car" _____ (be) seven miles an hour.

3. Although astronauts _____ (be) in outer space may times, they _____ (not/land) on any planets yet.

4. The first woman cosmonaut, Valentina Tereshkova, _____ (spend) seventy hours in space in 1963.

5. The United States _____ (launch) its first satellite in 1958 and since then we _____ (send) many different kinds of satellites into space.

6. In 1987, a Russian cosmonaut _____ (live) in a space station for 326 days. Imagine living in space for nearly a year!

7. Yuri Gagarin _____ (be) the first person in space, and Neil Armstrong and Buzz Aldrin _____ (be) the first to land on the moon.

**B. Write a question to go with each answer. Use present perfect or past tense.**

1. _*Who was the first person in space*_____ ?
   (Yuri Gagarin was.)

2. _____ ?
   (She spent 70 hours in space.)

3. _____ ?
   (Yes, they have.)

4. _____ ?
   (In 1969)

5. _____ ?
   (Armstrong and Aldrin were.)

6. _____ ?
   (For 362 days.)

**Skill Objectives: Contrasting present perfect and past tenses; asking questions.** Call attention to the grammar explanation at the top of the page. If students need more examples, provide them on the board. If students are still unsure about when to use the present perfect and when to use the past tense, go through all of Part A orally before assigning it for written work. *Part B:* Do the first two items as a class before assigning it for independent work.

74

# Word Skills: Irregular Plurals

Some plurals are difficult to form because of irregular spellings or because there are special rules for them. Look at the following rules for forming plurals. But be careful! There are many exceptions to these rules. Get into the habit of using your dictionary to check your work. It will give you the information you need about spelling irregularities and exceptions to the rules.

**Rule 1:** For words that end in a consonant followed by *y*, change the *y* to *i* and add *es* to form the plural. Example: *party, parties.*

**Rule 2:** For words that end in *sh, ch, x,* and *s*, add *es* to form the plural. Examples: *brush, brushes; church, churches; tax, taxes; kiss, kisses.*

**Rule 3:** For words that end in *f* or *fe*, change the *f* or *fe* to *v* and add *es.* Examples: *shelf, shelves; life, lives.* There are many exceptions to this rule.

**Rule 4:** Compound nouns form their plural by adding *s* to the most important word in the phrase. Example: *mother-in-law, mothers-in-law.*

**Rule 5:** For words that end in a consonant followed by *o*, add *es* to form the plural. Example: *potato, potatoes.* There are many exceptions to this rule, so check your dictionary.

**Rule 6:** Some words have special plural forms and do not take an *s* at all. Example: *man, men.*

**Rule 7:** Some words (mostly animal names) keep the same form in singular and plural. Example: *deer, deer.*

**Make the following words plural. Use your dictionary.**

1. thief _____
2. father-in-law _____
3. piano _____
4. penny _____
5. box _____
6. tooth _____
7. roof _____
8. tomato _____
9. mouse _____
10. scarf _____
11. moose _____
12. monkey _____

13. wife _____
14. foot _____
15. silo _____
16. wolf _____
17. sheep _____
18. chief _____
19. half _____
20. woman _____
21. pony _____
22. boss _____
23. wish _____
24. watch _____

**Skill Objectives: Constructing irregular plurals; using the dictionary to check spelling.** Review the rules with class, then assign the page for independent work. Have students correct their own work by using a dictionary.

75

# Our Closest Neighbor

Study a scientific article and answer questions about it.

**A. Make sure you know the meaning of the following important words which are underlined in the story.**

distance        plain        mankind        shuttle        galaxies
crater          shine        instruments    refueling      universe

**B. Read the story quickly to get some general ideas about it. Then read it again more slowly to answer the questions.**

## The Moon

The moon is our closest neighbor in the sky. It is only 239,000 miles away from us. Of course, that seems very far, but compared to the distance the Earth is from the sun or some of the other planets, it isn't much at all.

The moon is the Earth's satellite. It revolves or travels around the Earth. There are mountains, craters, and plains on the moon. Some of the moon's mountains are 15,000 feet high. The craters are large holes in the surface of the moon. The plains are gray, flat areas. Galileo, one of the first scientists to use a telescope to observe the moon, called the plains "seas" and "oceans."

The temperature on the moon can get as hot as 260°F. at noon and colder than –200°F. at night. During the day the sun shines on the moon. At night "earth-shine" lights up the moon. There is no air and no water on the moon. Scientists say that there never has been any life on the moon.

We learned a lot about the moon in 1959. Sputnik, a Soviet (Russian) space satellite, was the first to photograph the moon close up. Soon American rockets were traveling close to the moon. In July of 1969 the first human being walked on the moon. Neil Armstrong, an American, was the lucky person. He called his first step on the moon, "a small step for man; a giant leap for mankind." Armstrong and Edwin Aldrin picked up rocks and dirt from the moon and left recording instruments there.

American scientists believe that a trip to the moon is just the beginning of space exploration. They have developed the space shuttle, a rocket ship that can travel long distances, land, and after refueling take off again. Scientists want to send spaceships to other planets and other galaxies. Their goal is to explore the whole universe.

**C. Think carefully and answer the following question.**

Neil Armstrong called his first step on the moon "a giant step for mankind" because

a. he took a very large step.
b. it began a new chapter in space exploration.
c. the rocket ship he rode on was huge.
d. he was a hero and people called him a giant.

(Go on to the next page.)

**76**

**Skill Objectives: Reading comprehension; interpreting idiomatic expressions; building vocabulary.** Review the directions with the students. After the first reading, you may want to lead a discussion about the meaning of the highlighted vocabulary words. Encourage students to check and refine their definitions by using a dictionary.

**D. Circle the answer that best completes the sentence.**

The American government paid more attention to its space program in 1960 because

a. it wanted to know more about the moon.
b. the moon is our closest neighbor.
c. there is no air or water on the moon.
d. the Soviet Union sent its sputnik into space in 1959.

**E. Use a word from the underlined vocabulary to complete each of these sentences.**

1. I love to go out at night and see the stars _____.

2. The _____ from the earth to the sun is 93,000,000 miles.

3. I hope that there is peace for all _____ in the future.

4. The crew is _____ the plane before it takes off again.

5. There are several _____ in the universe.

**F. Use separate paper to write answers to these questions.**

1. How far is the moon from the earth?
2. How high are the mountains on the moon?
3. What are craters?
4. What did Galileo call the moon's plains?
5. What is the moon's hottest temperature?
6. How cold can the temperature get on the moon?
7. Why do scientists say there is no life on the moon?
8. What nation first photographed the moon close up?
9. Who was the first person to walk on the moon?
10. When did the first person walk on the moon?
11. What did that person say about the first step on the moon?
12. What did the astronauts pick up on the moon?
13. What did they leave behind?
14. Where else do scientists want to send spaceships?
15. What is the goal of these scientists?

**G. Number these events in the order in which they happened.**

_____ Armstrong and Aldrin walked on the moon.

_____ Galileo observed the moon with a telescope.

_____ American scientists developed the space shuttle.

_____ Russians took the first close-up pictures of the moon.

_____ American spaceships traveled close to the moon.

**H.** The story says that it is very hot on the moon "at noon," and very cold "at night." What is a lunar (moon) day? What is a lunar night? How long is each of these? How are they related to what we call a full moon, a new moon, etc.? On your paper write a paragraph or paragraphs answering these questions. Use an encyclopedia if you need to, but write your paragraph(s) in your own words.

**Skill Objectives: Reading for details; drawing inferences; sequencing; paraphrasing information from an encyclopedia.** Assign Parts C–G as independent work. Correct and discuss as a class. Have students use the encyclopedia or a science book to research the questions in Part H and bring their notes back for a classroom discussion. Help students organize the information they have gathered and restate the facts in their own words. Paraphrasing is a difficult skill. Present students with techniques, and provide lots of group practice.

77

# Library Catalog Cards

A library card catalog is a complete list, in card form, of the books owned by the library. To find out if the library owns a particular book, you look for that book in the catalog. To help you, the catalog has three kinds of cards for most books. There are author cards, which have the author's name at the top. There are title cards, which have the title of the book at the top. And there are subject cards, which have the subject of the book at the top. Often, all three cards are in the same set of catalog drawers. Sometimes, however, subject cards are in a separate set of drawers.

All the cards are filed alphabetically. Suppose you have a book called *Looking at the Moon*, by an author named John Adams. The author card will be filed with the A's.

The title card will be filed with the L's. And the subject card will be filed with the M's (for Moon). If you look under the M's, you will find other books on the same subject written by different authors. If you look under the A's, you will find other books by the same author, perhaps on different subjects. If you look under the L's, you will find other books whose titles start with "Look" or "Looking."

All the cards give you complete information about the book, including its title, its author(s), its publisher, and its subject. They also give you information about where it is located in the library. A "call number" in the upper left-hand corner of the card identifies the section of the library where the book is kept.

Look at the list below. These are the top lines from some catalog cards. **Tell which kind of card each one is. Write "author card," "title card," or "subject card" next to each one.**

1. RAILROADS _____

2. E.B. White _____

3. *Huckleberry Finn* _____

4. *Moby Dick* _____

5. PILGRIMS _____

6. CIVIL WAR _____

7. Madeleine L'Engle _____

8. F. Scott Fitzgerald _____

9. *The Call of the Wild* _____

10. SLAVERY _____

11. John Steinbeck _____

12. *For Whom the Bell Tolls* _____

13. *The Groucho Letters* _____

14. NEW YORK CITY _____

15. Ellen Goodman _____

16. *A Room of One's Own* _____

17. MOVIES _____

18. WITCHCRAFT _____

19. Emily Dickinson _____

20. *Pride and Prejudice* _____

```
522   Adams, John
A     Looking at the moon
      by John Adams.
```
```
522   Looking at the moon
A     by John Adams.
```
```
522   MOON
A     Looking at the moon
      by John Adams.
```

**Skill Objective: Using the card catalog.** Read and discuss the introduction together, then assign the exercises. Extension Activities: Have students use the card catalog to answer these questions: *1. Where are the subject cards filed in your library? 2. How many books can you find about railroads, the Pilgrims, movies, witchcraft? 3. Which books does your library have by the authors on this page? 4. Does your library have the books listed on this page? Write down the call numbers and locate the books on the shelves. 5. Does your library have its catalog on the computer? How is a computer catalog different from a card catalog?*

# The Future with "Will"

One way to talk about things that are going to happen in the future is to use the verb *will*. Look at the examples below.

I will graduate
He will ride
She will study
It will rain

You will leave
We will arrive
They will stay

You can use *will* with many future expressions such as the following:

next week
next month

next year
in a year

in a few days (weeks, months)
tomorrow

**A. Read the following paragraph and follow the instructions.**

We and our children will see many changes in the world in the next fifty years, just as our parents and grandparents have seen many changes in the past fifty years. Here are some of the kinds of changes some people think we will see:

1. We will drive electric cars.
2. We will find a cure for cancer and other diseases.
3. We will use solar energy in all our homes.
4. We will all have our own computers.
5. We will visit the moon for a vacation.
6. We will eat factory-made food.
7. We will travel by monorail in the cities.

What else do you think we will do in the next fifty years? Add three changes of your own.

8. _____

_____

9. _____

_____

10. _____

_____

**B. Now work with a classmate asking and answering questions from the ten changes above. Use the following model:**

—Do you think we will drive electric cars in the next fifty years?

—Yes, I think we will drive electric cars.

*or*

—No, I don't think we will drive electric cars.

**C. On your paper, write answers to these questions. Use complete sentences with *will*.**

1. When will you graduate from high school?
2. How old will you be on your next birthday?
3. What will you do this weekend?
4. Will you get a job or will you go to college after you graduate?
5. How old will you be when you get married?
6. When will your next school vacation begin?

**Skill Objective: Constructing the future tense with *will*.** Read the introductory paragraphs aloud. Ask students questions: *What will you do this afternoon/this weekend? When will you eat dinner tonight/have a vacation? Where will you travel someday/live ten years from now?* Assign Part A for independent work. Have students share their favorite answer. Circulate around the room as students practice Part B. Part C may be done in class or assigned for homework.

79

## Dear Dot

Dear Dot—

My sister Luisa keeps a diary. I know I was wrong, but one night when she left it on top of her desk I read it. Now I don't know what to do. Luisa met a boy two weeks ago, and he wants to marry her. She said no, but she wrote in her diary that every day she wants to go off with him a little bit more. You see, she's not happy at home. My parents nag her all the time because she gets bad grades in school. My problem is that if I ask my sister any questions, she will know that I read her diary. If I tell my mother, my sister will be very angry. What should I do?

Snoopy

1. Where did Luisa leave her diary? _____

_____

2. What is Luisa's secret? _____

_____

3. Why does she want to leave home? _____

_____

4. What is Snoopy's problem? _____

_____

5. What does the word *nag* mean in this letter? Circle the best answer.

   a. call and write     b. criticize     c. kiss and praise     d. old horse

6. What is your advice to Snoopy? Discuss your answer in class. Then play Dot's role and write a letter telling Snoopy what to do and what not to do.

   *Dear Snoopy* _____ ,

   _____

   _____

   _____

   _____

   _____

                                                    _____

**Skill Objectives: Reading for details; drawing conclusions; making judgments; writing a letter.** Have students read the letter and answer questions 1–5 independently. Correct these as a class. Then have students discuss question 6 and write their letters. Ask several volunteers to read their letters and have the class make suggestions for rephrasing, etc. As an additional option, you may want to have students write a page in a diary. They should make it a fantasy that they wish would come true. The page could begin, "Dear Diary, a fantastic thing happened to me today . . ."

# What Did She Tell You?

**Complete the conversations.** The first one and the fourth one are done for you.

1. Please wash the dishes. — What did she tell you? — She told me to wash the dishes.

2. Please make your bed. — What did he tell you? — He _____ _____ _____

3. Please mow the lawn! — What did she tell you? — She _____ _____ _____

4. Set the table. — What did he ask you to do? — He asked me to set the table.

5. Mail this letter, please. — What did she ask you to do? — She _____ _____ _____

6. Do your homework! — What did they tell you? — They _____ _____ _____

7. Meet me in the cafeteria! — What did she want you to do? — She _____ _____ _____

**Skill Objective: Reporting a speech.** Write commands on pieces of paper. *Read your book. Go away. Hurry up. etc.* Write on the board, *What did he/she tell you?* Have a volunteer whisper a written command to you. The class will ask, "What did he/she tell you?" Model the answer, "She told me to . . ." Have students come up in pairs. Hand a command to one student and practice these structures. Assign the page as independent work.

# The Present Perfect Progressive Tense

The present perfect progressive tense is used for activities that *began sometime in the past and continue up to the present.* Time expressions with *for* and *since* usually use this tense. Look at these examples of the present perfect progressive.

I
You
We
They } have been living here. { for 2 years.
since 1987.

He
She
It } has been living here { for many years.
since May.

The examples below compare the present perfect progressive with the past and present.

PAST: I started to study English two months ago.
PRESENT: I am studying English now.
PRESENT PERFECT PROGRESSIVE: I have been studying English for two months.

**A.** The two boxes tell you when to use *for* and when to use *since*. **Read them, then complete the sentences under them using *for* or *since*.**

Use *for* with general time words that describe a period or length of time, but don't give an exact date or time when an action started. For example:

I have been living here . . .
   *for* a few years.
   *for* a month.
   *for* a couple of weeks.
   *for* three hours.
   *for* all my life.

Use *since* with specific time words that tell when an action started, or with phrases that also tell when an action started. For example:

I have been living here . . .
   *since* 1975.
   *since* February.
   *since* March 19th.
   *since* 6:00 P.M.
   *since* I was a young girl.

1. Susan has been working at the bank _____ years.

2. I have been waiting for you _____ 3:30.

3. Jose has been talking on the phone _____ two hours.

4. Mr. and Mrs. Chang have been living in Baltimore _____ 1986.

5. It has been raining _____ last night.

6. Mr. Steinberg has been teaching _____ he graduated from college.

7. You have been studying English _____ a long time.

8. Europeans have been coming to the Americas _____ the 15th century.

9. Trang has been driving _____ she was 16 years old.

10. The telephone has been ringing _____ two minutes.

11. We have been sitting in this class _____ an hour.

12. I have been thinking about you _____ a long time.

13. Pablo has been working on my portrait _____ last July.

14. That castle has been standing _____ several centuries.

15. The wreath has been on the door _____ December.

16. It has been raining _____ almost a month.

(Go on to the next page.)

**Skill Objective: Describing periods of time with *for* and *since*.** Call attention to the grammar explanation at the top of the page. Go over the construction of the present perfect progressive. Provide more examples on the board, eliciting them from the class. *Part A:* Read the boxes explaining the uses of *for* and *since*, then ask a student, *How long have you been (living in _____ /studying English/working at _____ )?* The student may answer with *for* or *since*: be sure he/she uses them correctly. Then assign the sixteen items for independent work.

**B. Write the sentences in the present perfect progressive form.** The first one is done for you.

1. Americans started wearing nylon clothing in 1938.
   *Americans have been wearing nylon clothing since 1938.*

2. Astronauts started traveling in outer space in 1961.

3. People started using computers in 1959.

4. Americans started flying in airplanes in 1903.

5. McDonald's started selling hamburgers in 1955.

6. Students started studying at Harvard University in 1636.

**C. Read about Luis, and answer the questions using the correct tense.**

| | |
|---|---|
| May, 1987 | came to the United States from Guatemala |
| June, 1987 | started English classes |
| July, 1987 | started working at a gas station |
| March, 1988 | met Amelia |
| May, 1988 | completed English classes |
| June, 1988 | quit his job at gas station |
| July, 1988 | started job at a bank |
| March, 1989 | married Amelia |

1. How long has Luis been living in the United States?

2. How long did he study English?

3. How long did he work at the gas station?

4. When did he meet Amelia?

5. How long has he been working at the bank?

6. How long have Luis and Amelia been married?

7. How long has Luis known Amelia?

**Skill Objective: Writing sentences with present perfect progressive.** *Part B:* Do the first two items orally with the class, then assign the others as independent work. *Part C:* Do the first two items together before assigning the others as independent work. Be sure students understand that their answers should be based on the biographical data about Luis.

83

# Answering Questions Correctly

Pay attention to the question words in a sentence in order to answer them in the correct tense. Look at the following examples.

---

### AFFIRMATIVE (YES)

| | |
|---|---|
| Does she live in Texas? | Yes, she lives in Texas. |
| Is she living in Texas? | Yes, she's living in Texas. |
| Did she live in Texas? | Yes, she lived in Texas. |
| Was she living in Texas? | Yes, she was living in Texas. |
| Will she live in Texas? | Yes, she will live in Texas. |
| Has she been living in Texas? | Yes, she has been living in Texas. |

### NEGATIVE (NO)

| | |
|---|---|
| Do they work in Ohio? | No, they don't work in Ohio. |
| Are they working in Ohio? | No, they aren't working in Ohio. |
| Did they work in Ohio? | No, they didn't work in Ohio. |
| Were they working in Ohio? | No, they weren't working in Ohio. |
| Will they work in Ohio? | No, they won't work in Ohio. |
| Have they been working in Ohio? | No, they haven't been working in Ohio. |

### OTHER

| | |
|---|---|
| What school do you go to? | I go to Adams School. |
| What school are you going to now? | I'm going to Adams School now. |
| What school did you go to? | I went to Adams School. |
| What school were you going to then? | I was going to Adams School then. |
| What school will you go to? | I will go to Adams School. |
| What school have you been going to? | I have been going to Adams School. |

---

**Make up answers to the following questions and write them on your paper. Make sure you use the same tense in both the question and the answer.**

1. Have you been listening to the radio for a long time?
2. Where did Mark find his shoe?
3. When are you leaving?
4. What has the dog been doing all day?
5. Will your brother enjoy this book?
6. Do you eat liver?
7. Are you living in Arizona now?
8. When did you meet the Wilsons?
9. When will you decide about going on vacation?
10. How many people were living in that apartment?
11. Does this restaurant serve pizza?
12. Have you been paying your bills this year?
13. Were they driving all day yesterday?
14. Do you have a lot of money in the bank?
15. Did the glass fall on the floor?
16. Were you making a lot of money when you worked in Chicago?
17. Will you call the theater to find out when the play starts?
18. How long have you been keeping this secret for?
19. When did you take your friend to the hospital?
20. Will they apply to college in January?
21. Were your cousins buying a new car when I saw them?
22. How long have you been feeling sick?
23. When will your boss increase your salary?
24. Does the bus driver give change?
25. Which color suit did you choose?

**Skill Objective: Reviewing present, past, future, and present perfect progressive tenses.** Be sure students understand the differences between the tenses. A rapid-fire oral drill requiring students to use short answers *(Yes, I did/No, she wasn't)* can be fun, especially if you write or ask questions appropriate to your students. After doing the first two items together, assign the page as independent work.

# How Long and How Many?

**Use complete sentences to answer the questions.** The first one is done for you.

**1990**
**200,000 miles**

Fran is a truck driver. She started driving a truck last year and she is driving a truck today.

*How long* has she been *driving* a truck? __She has been driving__
__a truck for one year.__ _____ (TIME)

*How many* miles has she *driven* in the past year? __She has driven__
__200,000 miles in the past year.__ _____ (QUANTITY)

**1987**
**3 books**

Lisa is a writer. She started writing books in 1987, and she is writing today.

*How long* has she been *writing* books? _____

_____

*How many* books has she *written* since 1987? _____

_____

**1969**
**1600 students**

Henry and Roberta are teachers. They both started teaching in 1969 and they are teaching today.

*How long* have they been *teaching*? _____

_____

*How many* students have they *taught* since 1969? _____

_____

**1964**
**401 homes**

We are real estate salesmen. We started selling houses in 1958. We are selling houses today.

*How long* have we been *selling* homes? _____

_____

*How many* houses have we *sold* since 1964? _____

_____

**1931**
**3000 pairs**

I am a shoemaker. I started making shoes in 1931. I am making shoes today.

*How long* have I been *making* shoes? _____

_____

*How many* pairs of shoes have I *made* since 1931? _____

_____

**Skill Objective: Comparing present perfect progressive and present perfect.** Read the first example with the class. Have a volunteer explain why the present perfect continuous is used in the first question and the present perfect in the second question. Assign the page as independent work. Extension Activity: Have students draw portraits and write similar "stories" and questions about other progressionals (a surgeon, two cooks, an explorer, etc.) Their classmates can read the stories and answer the questions.

85

# An Important Science

**A. Make sure you know the meaning of the following important words which are underlined in the story.**

| | | | | |
|---|---|---|---|---|
| complicated | molecules | escape | examine | rusty |
| principles | attract | split | substance | sour |
| matter | collection | atoms | combine | |

**B. Read the story quickly to get some general ideas about it. Then read it again more slowly to answer the questions.**

## Chemistry

Many students feel that chemistry is a difficult subject. They are so afraid of the challenge of chemistry that they don't take the time to learn anything about it. It is true that chemistry is a complicated subject, but there are some ideas and principles of chemistry that everyone can and should understand. They are:

1. All matter (all things) is made up of small separate particles called molecules.
2. Molecules move very fast and they are always moving.
2. Molecules attract each other.

Let's look at an example of these three rules. A bottle of ammonia is a collection of ammonia molecules. If you open a bottle of ammonia in a closed room, the smell is everywhere in the room. Why? Some molecules of ammonia (remember molecules are very small and you can't see them) have escaped from the bottle and are flying through the air. They cause the smell.

Why don't all of the molecules fly out of the bottle? Remember rule number three. Molecules attract each other. Most of the molecules don't escape because they are attracted to, or pulled toward, each other.

Molecules are not the smallest particles of matter. Scientists can split the molecule into smaller particles called atoms. Chemistry is the study of molecules and atoms. Chemists examine different substances and find out about their molecules and atoms. Chemists combine molecules of one substance with molecules of another. They want to see what changes take place.

Why does a nail, left outside, get rusty? Why does bread rise when you bake it? Why does milk get sour? These are all chemical changes. If you want to know what causes these chemical changes, why not try a chemistry course? Chemistry is complicated but it is also rewarding. It explains many of the occurences of day-to-day living.

**C. Think carefully and answer the following question.**

The rules and principles of chemistry try to explain

a. why ammonia smells.
b. why atoms are smaller than molecules.
c. the behavior and makeup of matter.
d. how fast molecules move.

(Go on to the next page.)

**Skill Objectives: Reading comprehension; identifying main idea; building vocabulary.** Review the directions with the students. After the first reading, you may want to lead a discussion about the meaning of the highlighted vocabulary words. Encourage students to check and refine their definitions by using a dictionary.

**D. Circle the answer that best completes the sentence.**

According to this article, a sliced onion makes you cry because

a. the knife splits the atoms.
b. the molecules attract each other.
c. some molecules escape and reach the eyes.
d. the molecules move very fast.

**E. Use a word from the underlined vocabulary to complete each of these sentences.**

1. Ramon has an interesting _____ of butterflies.

2. I can't understand these directions; they're too _____.

3. The milk doesn't taste good; I think it's _____.

4. Two prisoners tried to _____ from jail last week.

5. Artists _____ colors to make new and different shades.

**F. Use separate paper to write answers to these questions.**

1. Why are many students afraid of chemistry?

2. What is the smallest particle of matter mentioned in the story?

3. What do chemists do?

4. Why do chemists combine molecules of different substances?

5. Why is chemistry rewarding?

**G. Certain things cause certain other things to happen. Look at the causes at the left. Find the effect at the right that goes with each cause, and write its letter in the blank for that cause. Use your dictionary for words you don't know.**

1. too many automobiles in a city _____        a. damage and destruction

2. drinking too much alcohol _____             b. sourness

3. vitamin deficiency _____                    c. temporary pain relief

4. tornado _____                               d. drunkenness

5. taking aspirin tablets _____                e. sickness and body malfunction

6. leaving a nail outdoors _____               f. air pollution

7. leaving milk out of the refrigerator _____  g. rust

**H. Find out what the word *synthetic* means. What does this have to do with chemistry? Use an encyclopedia to find out some of the common things around you that have been developed by chemists. Take notes, then write a paragraph telling the facts you have learned in your own words.**

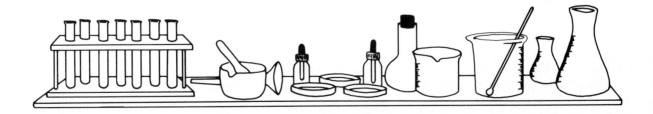

Skill Objectives: Reading for details; drawing conclusions; understanding cause and effect; researching; writing a report. Assign Parts C–G as independent work. Discuss the assignment in Part H. Ask students where they will look to find the meaning of *synthetic*. What entry will they look up in the encyclopedia (chemists, chemistry, synthetics)? Will they need to read the entire article? Remind students to use the headings to skim the article until they come to the section that contains the specific information they are looking for.

# Martha Miller

Last month, Martha Miller won $10,000 in the state lottery. She has decided to take a vacation to Paris, France. Paris is a place she has always wanted to visit. She has been very busy lately making plans for her trip. She plans to leave next month.

Martha has been calling a few travel agents. In the past month she has called three agents. She wants to know more about Paris, so she has been reading a few books about that city. In the past month, she has read two books.

Martha also wants to be able to speak the language, so she has been taking French lessons at the university. In the past month, she has taken eight lessons. She has been shopping for some new clothes, too. She has shopped in some of the best stores in her city. She has also been making new clothes. She has already made a skirt, and a blouse.

As you can see, Martha has been having a good time getting ready for her trip. Sometimes, getting ready for a vacation is half the fun!

**A. Write questions about the story to fit the answers at the right.** The first one is done for you.

1. How much _did Martha Miller win_? She won $10,000.

2. Where _____? She has decided to go to France.

3. Why _____? She has always wanted to go there.

4. When _____? She plans to leave in a month.

5. Who _____? She's been calling a few travel agents.

6. How many _____? She's called three agents so far.

7. What _____? She's been reading a few books about Paris.

8. How many _____? She has read two books so far.

9. Why _____? She wants to know more about Paris.

10. Where _____? She has been taking French at the university.

11. Has _____? Yes, she has.

12. What _____? She's made a skirt and a blouse.

13. Has _____? No, she hasn't.

14. _____? _____

**B. On your paper, write five true or false statements about the story.** For example: Martha Miller won $50,000 (false). She is going to take a vacation in Paris (true).

**Skill Objectives: Reviewing present perfect progressive and present perfect; simple past; *plans to/wants to*; constructing questions.** Have students read the story silently, then discuss and construct the first few questions as a class. Remind students to pay close attention to the verb tense used in the answer. Assign the page as independent work.

# Word Skills: Category Labels

Look at each list of words below. Decide how the words on the list are the same, and think of a word or phrase that names or labels the list. Write the word or phrase in the blank. Use your dictionary or other books if you need to. The first list is labeled for you.

1. _____ languages _____ Spanish, Chinese, Italian, Vietnamese, English

2. _____ Monopoly, chess, checkers, dominoes, Scrabble

3. _____ piano, guitar, drums, saxophone, string bass

4. _____ lily, petunia, rose, daisy, daffodil

5. _____ sofa, chair, table, bed, dresser

6. _____ wash clothes, iron, do dishes, empty trash, sweep

7. _____ Christmas, New Year, Independence Day, Thanksgiving

8. _____ poodle, collie, dalmation, German shepherd, spaniel

9. _____ penny, nickel, dime, quarter, half-dollar

10. _____ novel, dictionary, encyclopedia, Bible, atlas

11. _____ Saturn, Neptune, Pluto, Mars, Mercury

12. _____ dog, cat, fish, bird, hamster

13. _____ sparrow, robin, blue jay, eagle, pigeon

14. _____ Carson City, Austin, Sacramento, Albany, Helena

15. _____ trout, salmon, cod, shark, mackerel

16. _____ ant, grasshopper, fly, bee, cockroach

17. _____ North America, South America, Europe, Africa, Asia

18. _____ Capricorn, Leo, Aries, Pisces, Libra

19. _____ Mary, Ruth, Betty, Lisa, Rita

20. _____ bacon, lettuce, and tomato; ham and cheese; tuna fish; peanut butter and jelly; grilled cheese

**Skill Objective: Classifying.** Assign this page for independent work. Correct and discuss as a class.

89

# She and Him and They and Them

The subject of a sentence is the person or thing doing something. The object is the person or thing to whom or for whom the thing is done. Often the subjects or objects are pronouns. Look at the following example:

Jose gave his book to Marla.
He gave his book to her.

Here are the English subject and object pronouns:

| Subject pronouns | Object pronouns |
|---|---|
| I | me |
| you | you |
| he | him |
| she | her |
| it | it |
| we | us |
| they | them |

**A. Make up answers to the questions. In your answers, replace the underlined words with object pronouns.** The first one is done for you.

1. What did you ask Robert?

   *I asked him to be quiet.*

2. What did the teacher tell the children?

   _____

3. What did those women ask you and me?

   _____

4. What did Rajiv tell his mother?

   _____

5. What did Mr. Adler ask the waiter?

   _____

6. What did the driver do to the lamp post?

   _____

**B. Circle the correct pronoun for each sentence.** The first one is done for you.

1. John will meet (we, us) at the theater.
2. I have already played chess with (they, them).
3. (I, Me) get a lot of vitamin A.
4. Do you want (he, him) to leave now?
5. (She, Her) had a summer job at the bakery.
6. I'm going to take (they, them) to the airport.
7. Tell (he, him) to turn down the radio.
8. I had a long talk with (she, her) and her sister.

**Skill Objective: Reviewing subject and object pronouns.** Go over the grammar explanation in the box at the top of the page. Do Parts A and B together orally if you believe students will have difficulty with them. Otherwise assign the page as independent work.

## Dear Dot

Dear Dot—

    I bought my girlfriend an expensive necklace for her birthday. She liked it, but she wouldn't accept it. She told me that her mother taught her not to accept such expensive presents from someone she was not engaged to. I am very disappointed. I want her to have this necklace, and I don't care about some silly rule of etiquette that says otherwise. Dot, does that old rule really matter anymore?

Diamond Jim

1. What did Jim buy his girlfriend for her birthday? _____
   _____

2. Why didn't his girlfriend accept the gift? _____
   _____

3. How does Jim feel about the situation? _____
   _____

4. What does Jim want? _____

5. What does the word *silly* mean in this letter? Circle the best answer.

   a. foolish    b. old    c. friendly    d. careful

6. What is your advice to Jim? Discuss your answer in class. Then take Dot's role and write a letter to Jim answering his question.

   _____ ,

   _____

   _____

   _____

   _____

   _____

   _____

   _____

**Skill Objectives: Reading for details; drawing conclusions; making judgments; writing a letter.** Have students read the letter and answer questions 1-5 independently. Correct these as a class. Then have students discuss question 6 and write their letters. Ask several volunteers to read their letters, and have the class make suggestions for rephrasing, etc. As an additional option, have students write a paragraph about some of the rules of "etiquette" that were a part of their upbringing.

91

# Something, Anything

*Some* and *any* are called indefinite adjectives because they refer to an amount or quantity that is not definite or specific. *Somebody, anybody, something,* and *anything* are called indefinite pronouns because they do not name or refer to definite or particular persons or things. **Complete each of the sentences by filling each blank with one of the following indefinite adjectives or pronouns: *some, any, somebody, anybody, something, anything.*** The first one is done for you.

1. She doesn't have _____*any*_____ money in her account.

2. There are _____ students from China in my class.

3. I don't think _____ has seen her recently.

4. There aren't _____ students in my class from Russia.

5. Shhh! I think I hear _____ in the next room.

6. _____ ate my lunch!

7. May I have _____ more tea, please.

8. I wanted to borrow _____ money from her but she said that she didn't have _____.

9. She never gives her poor cat _____ milk to drink.

10. The police asked me _____ questions but I didn't know _____.

11. I didn't have _____ milk, so I went to the store to buy _____.

12. I entered the room but I didn't see _____ so I left.

13. I thought I heard a noise in the next room but my wife didn't hear _____.

14. It's my mother's birthday tomorrow, so I have to go out and buy her _____.

15. There is _____ wrong with my bike.

16. Mr. Villalba never gives his wife _____ money.

17. The baby is hungry so I'm giving her _____ to eat.

18. David didn't want _____ to eat.

19. _____ just telephoned you; he's going to call back later.

20. I have _____ to tell you.

**Skill Objective: Using indefinite pronouns and adjectives.** Teach/review the indefinite adjectives and pronouns asking, "Do you have any (some) questions?" ("*No,* I don't have *any* questions./*Yes,* I have *some* questions.") "Is there anybody (somebody) in the hall? Do I have anything (something) behind my back?" Note that negative statements use *any, anybody, anything,* and positive statements use *some, somebody,* and *something.* Questions can use either form. Do the first few items on this page as a class, then assign for independent work.

# I Just Ate!

The word *just* has several meanings. One meaning of *just* is "recently in the past." It is used with the past tense or the present perfect tense. "I just ate" and "I have just eaten" both mean "I finished eating a few minutes ago." **Use the word *just* in your answers to the questions below.** The first two are done for you. Use them as models for the others.

1. Why is John upset?

*John is upset because his dog has just eaten part of the rug.*

2. Why is Lisa happy?

*Lisa is happy because she just won $1000 in the lottery.*

3. Why is Christina happy?

4. Why is Rolando upset?

5. Why is Mrs. Poleo mad?

6. Why is Alexis happy?

7. Why is Carla sad?

8. Why are Mr. and Mrs. Soto happy?

9. Why is Mr. Nguyen upset?

**Skill Objective: Using *just* with present perfect and simple past.** Whisper to a student, "Write on the board." Then ask, "What did s(he) just do?" If needed, prompt answer, "She just wrote on the board." Direct another student to erase the board and ask, "What has he just done?" If needed, provide additional situations for oral practice. Go over the first two items together. Point out that either the simple past or the present perfect can be used. Assign as independent work.

# Why Did It Happen?

Often you have to explain to someone why something happened. In the exercise below, there are *results*—what actually happened—in Column I and *causes*—why the things happened—in Column II.

**A. Match the causes in Column II with the results in Column I by writing the letter of the cause next to the result.** The first one is done for you.

Column I: Results

1. I lost my money __q__
2. They got wet _____
3. He tripped _____
4. We sank _____
5. The cat scratched itself _____
6. We said thank you _____
7. We bought a turkey _____
8. I sent May a valentine _____
9. The dog wagged its tail _____
10. Bob yawned _____
11. I zipped my jacket _____
12. I took a deep breath _____
13. We turned on the fan _____
14. Tim got a flashlight _____
15. Bill frowned _____
16. Mike guessed the answer _____
17. We put on masks and costumes _____
18. The boys shook hands _____
19. We didn't catch a fish _____
20. The baby sat on my lap _____

Column II: Causes

a. Thanksgiving was coming
b. the weather was cool and windy
c. it was so happy
d. he was going out in the dark
e. I wanted to stay under water for 20 seconds
f. he had no idea what it was
g. they forgot to bring their umbrellas
h. they wanted the fight to be finished and forgotten
i. it had fleas
j. there was no hook on our line
k. he didn't see the bumps in the rug
l. there was no extra chair for her
m. he didn't like the grade he got on his test
n. someone bought us a gift
o. I'm in love with her
p. it was a hot, sticky day
q. I had a hole in my pocket
r. he was tired and wanted to go
s. there were holes in the bottom of the boat
t. it was Halloween night

**B. Now write ten of the sentences you have matched, joining them with the word *because*.**

> Example: I lost my money because I had a hole in my pocket.

**Skill Objectives: Determining cause and effect; writing sentences.** Explain the directions to students and go over any new vocabulary. Do the first three items together, then assign the page as independent work.

# Using Reference Books

A reference book is a book designed to provide information on one or more subjects. Dictionaries and encyclopedias are reference books. There are many other kinds of reference books, too. Some of these are described below. **Look at the descriptions and use them to help you complete the page.**

### Some Reference Books

*Almanac:* a yearly publication that includes lists, charts and tables, and summaries of information in many unrelated fields.

*Atlas:* a collection of maps; atlases often also include population statistics.

*Book of Quotations:* a listing of well-known quotations from authors, politicians, and other famous people. The quotations are indexed to make them easy to find.

*Facts on File:* a bimonthly summary of major stories in more than fifty United States and foreign newspapers. Complete indexes make stories easy to locate.

*Thesaurus:* a book of synonyms and antonyms.

*Readers' Guide to Periodical Literature:* an author/subject index of articles and stories in a large number of magazines published in the United States. It comes out twice a month (once a month in certain months).

**Now look at the topics below. Tell which of the reference books described above you might use to find more information about the subject. Include the dictionary and encyclopedia.** The first one is done for you.

1. the height of Mount Shasta     *atlas (or almanac, encyclopedia)*
2. synonyms for the word *run* _____
3. maps of the Central Plains states _____
4. riots in London last summer _____
5. who wrote "To be or not to be . . ." _____
6. the opposite of *careful* _____
7. recent developments in bilingual education _____
8. rainfall in Tokyo _____
9. antonyms for the word *happy* _____
10. source of "A penny saved is a penny earned." _____
11. current population of Senegal _____
12. a series of recent murders in New York City _____
13. another word meaning *laugh* _____
14. articles about track competition _____
15. last month's elections in Honduras _____
16. the origin and different meanings of *rich* _____
17. all magazine articles by John Updike _____
18. maps of all the countries of Europe _____
19. brief biographies of the Presidents _____
20. the origin and history of the metric system _____

**Skill Objective: Comparing the uses of different reference books.** Have students read the information at the top of the page. Ask questions to check comprehension. Remind students that they can also refer to the dictionary and encyclopedia to find information. Sometimes information can be found in several sources. Do the first few items as a class, then assign as independent work. Extension Activity: Have students use the appropriate reference books to find the answers to some of the queries.

95

# Here To Stay (1)

**A. Make sure you know the meaning of the following important words which are underlined in the story.**

settled          continent          established          failed
descendants      actually           disappeared          rough

**B. Read the story quickly to get some general ideas about it. Then read it again more slowly to answer the questions.**

## The East Coast

About 35,000 years ago, some Asian hunters walked across Alaska and settled in what is now the United States. At that time, Asia and Alaska were connected by land. The Indians or Native Americans are the descendants of these Asian hunters. As far as anyone knows they were the first people to live in North America. For thousands of years the Indians were the only people to live on the continent. In 1492, things changed. On October 12th of that year, Christopher Columbus discovered "the new world." Within a few years of his discovery, thousands of Europeans sailed across the Atlantic Ocean to exlore the new world. Many of these explorers settled in North America.

The Spanish were the first Europeans to actually live in North America. In 1565, Pedro Menendez de Aviles and his men established the first North American city. They called it Saint Augustine. Many people go to Florida to visit Saint Augustine every year.

The English were the next group of Europeans to live in North America. In 1584, Sir Walter Raleigh established a settlement on Roanoke Island off the coast of what is now North Carolina. He was the leader of a hundred men and women. It was on this island that Virginia Dare was born. She was the first English child born in the new world.

Unfortunately, Virginia Dare and the other citizens of Roanoke Island disappeared one day. No one knows exactly what happened to these people. It is one of the great mysteries of early North American history.

The first successful English settlement in North America was Jamestown in Virginia. Captain John Smith was the leader of the Jamestown settlement. Jamestown almost failed too, but Pocahontas, an Indian woman, saved the life of Captain Smith and convinced the Indians to make peace with the English settlers. After a few difficult years, Jamestown became a rich and lively city.

In 1620, a boat called the *Mayflower* landed about 300 miles north of Jamestown. The people on the boat, the Pilgrims, called their new town Plymouth. They had a difficult time at first, but with the help of friendly Indians, they survived the rough winters and became successful.

After the success of Jamestown and Plymouth, more people decided to move to the new world. At first they settled close to the original settlements, Plymouth and Jamestown. Soon, however, they moved to other parts of the continent. Almost everyone who traveled to North America remained. The early settlers were here to stay.

**C. Think carefully and answer the following question.**

For the most part, people who left Europe for the New World were
a. fierce and foolish.
b. old and sick.
c. brave and adventurous.
d. sad and lonely.

(Go on to the next page.)

**Skill Objectives: Reading comprehension; inferring character traits; building vocabulary.** Review the directions with the students. After the first reading, you may want to lead a discussion about the meaning of the highlighted vocabulary words. Encourage students to check and refine their definitions by using a dictionary. Display a U.S. and world map. Have students locate the places mentioned in the reading. Extension Activity: Help students outline the information in the second through fifth paragraphs: *I. Spanish settlements* and *II. English settlements*.

**D. You can often guess what happened from the facts you read. Decide which of the answers best completes the sentence, and circle it.**

The people of Roanoke Island probably

a. died at the hands of the Indians.
b. returned to England.
c. sailed to Saint Augustine.
d. moved to Jamestown.

**E. Use a word from the underlined vocabulary to complete each of these sentences.**

1. James had to repeat Algebra I; he _____ it last term.

2. Asia is the largest _____.

3. The kidnapped children _____ a week ago.

4. My grandparents _____ in Puerto Rico fifty years ago.

5. Things weren't easy for me last year; I had a very _____ time.

**F. Number the statements in the order in which they happened.** The number 1 is done for you.

_____ Virginia Dare was born.

_____ The Pilgrims landed at Plymouth.

__1__ Asians walked across to Alaska and settled in what is now the United States.

_____ The Spanish established the city of Saint Augustine.

_____ The British established a settlement on Roanoke Island.

_____ Captain John Smith led a group of settlers to Jamestown.

_____ Christopher Columbus sailed across the Atlantic Ocean.

**G. Match the speakers with the quotation that fits best by writing the letter of the quotation in the blank next to the speaker's name.**

1. Christopher Columbus _____
2. Pedro Menendez de Aviles _____
3. Sir Walter Raleigh _____
4. John Smith _____
5. Pocahontas _____

a. "As the leader of the Jamestown colony, I insist that everyone work hard."

b. "Men, we have finally reached land! We are the first to discover a new route to a distant land."

c. "We have to help these strange people, father. They will die without us."

d. "We will call our new city Saint Augustine."

e. "The settlers of Roanoke Island are the bravest people to come to the New World."

**H. Use an encyclopedia to find out about some of the other leaders who established settlements on the east coast: New Netherlands, Massachusetts Bay, Rhode Island, Connecticut, Pennsylvania, Maryland, and Georgia. On your paper write a paragraph about one of these settlements and its leader(s).**

---

**Skill Objectives: Predicting outcomes; making inferences; sequencing; researching and writing a short report.** *Part H:* New Netherlands, Massachusetts Bay, Rhode Island, Connecticut, Pennsylvania, Maryland, and Georgia were other early East Coast settlements. Have students locate these places on a map, then choose one to research. Remind students to skim encyclopedia articles to find the section about the topic they are interested in, take notes, then individually or as a group, write a report.

# It's Your Choice

**A.** Sometimes the present perfect tense is used to describe things that have a "present" meaning—things that are happening at the present time. Sometimes it is used with a "past" meaning, to describe things that are not happening at the present time but did happen in the past. **Read the sentences below. Decide if the sentence has a present or a past meaning and write *present* or *past* in the blank.** The first two are done for you.

1. ___*present*___ I have been in the United States for two months. (I am here now.)

2. ___*past*___ I have been to New York City twice. (I went there in the past.)

3. _____ Ramon has already seen that movie.

4. _____ You have worked at that store for three months.

5. _____ They have worked at many jobs.

6. _____ I have known Trang since 1987.

7. _____ I have read that book before.

8. _____ Michiko has had her driver's license since she was 16.

9. _____ He has had three operations on his knee.

10. _____ Lucienne has been teaching French for a long time.

11. _____ Spiro and Galina have recently graduated from college.

12. _____ They have studied English since last August.

**B.** **Complete each sentence with either the past or the present perfect tense of the verb in parentheses.** The first two are done for you.

1. McDonald's ___*has sold*___ (sell) billions of hamburgers since they opened in 1955.

2. Our teacher ___*gave*___ (give) us two tests last month!

3. When Robert was in France, he _____ (see) the movie *Cousin Cousine* three times.

4. Yoshiko _____ (see) the movie *Star Wars* three times, and she plans to see it again.

5. The president of the United States _____ (meet) with the prime minister of England last week.

6. Cathy and Mike are taking guitar lessons. They _____ (take) them for a year.

**Skill Objective: Contrasting present perfect with present and past tenses.** *Part A:* Explain the directions carefully and provide examples on the board if students have difficulty grasping the concept. Do all the items orally before having students write them if you believe students need this help. *Part B:* This is a review of the distinction between present perfect and past tenses. Do all items orally if you believe students still need this help.

# Word Skills: Analogies

An analogy is a comparison between two sets of words. To complete an analogy, you must discover the relationship between the words in the first set, and then find a word that makes that same relationship with the first word in the other set. When you are completing the analogies on this page, think about the word skills you have already practiced in this book: synonyms, antonyms, homophones, and categories. These are some of the ways in which words in an analogy can relate to each other. Look at the example below. Choose one of the four answers.

big : little :: old : _____

small    tall    young    quiet

The correct answer is *young*. *Big* and *little* are antonyms, so you must find an antonym for *old*; the only one given is *young*.

(NOTE: You read the analogy as "Big is to little as old is to young.")

**Now complete each of the following analogies. Circle your answers.**

1. breakfast : morning :: lunch : _____ meal afternoon dinner eat

2. banana : yellow :: apple : _____ food fruit fresh red

3. mouse : mice :: tooth : _____ mouth white animal teeth

4. wall : clock :: wrist : _____ time arm watch o'clock

5. to : too :: write : _____ wrote paper right wrong

6. bottom : top :: cellar : _____ attic basement house down

7. doctor : hospital :: professor : _____ subject university teacher lawyer

8. blood : red :: sugar : _____ sweet color salt white

9. up : down :: in : _____ into on out from

10. glove : hand :: sock : _____ shoe foot leg punch

11. winter : cold :: summer : _____ hot season sun fever

12. ring : finger :: bracelet : _____ jewelry arm neck chest

13. oak : tree :: rose : _____ woman red pink flower

14. chauffeur : car :: pilot : _____ airplane airport fly runway

15. fight : fought :: shoot : _____ gun shot enemy west

16. bad : awful :: good : _____ better wonderful terrible best

17. chemistry : science :: geometry : _____ mathematics algebra subject Greek

18. film : movie :: cheap : _____ costly store sale inexpensive

**Skill Objective: Completing analogies.** Complete the first few items as a class. Let students explain the relationship by putting the word pairs in a sentence, "You eat *breakfast* in the *morning* and you eat *lunch* in the *afternoon*." Assign the page as independent work. Extension Activity: Students may enjoy creating and exchanging their own analogies.

99

# Two Careers

Look at the chart below. It gives you information about the careers of two people. **Use this information to answer the questions.**

| Name | Place of Birth | Date of Birth | Came to U.S.A. | Address in U.S.A | Degrees | College | Occupation Now |
|------|------|------|------|------|------|------|------|
| Amin Jabbour | Beirut, Lebanon | 5/14/60 | 1/5/81 | Quincy, MA 1981–1984 | B.S. 1984 (civil engineering) | Northeastern University | Professor of Civil Engineering at the University of Texas 1986– |
| | | | | Boston, MA 1984–1986 | M.S. 1986 (civil engineering) | Mass. Inst. of Technology (MIT) | |
| | | | | Austin, TX 1986– | | | |
| Isabel Minton | Leeds, England | 5/3/55 | | | B.A. 1977 (psychology) | Univ. of Manchester | Psychologist in Bristol, England 1984– |
| | | | | | M.A. 1981 (psychology) | University of London | Married 1987 |
| | | | | | Ph.D. 1984 (psychology) | University of London | |

NOTE: MA is the standard post office abbreviation for Massachusetts. TX is the standard post office abbreviation for Texas.

**A. Answer the questions about Professor Jabbour on your paper. Use complete sentences.**

1. Where was Professor Jabbour born?
2. When was he born?
3. Has he ever been to the U.S.A.?
4. When did he come to the U.S.A.?
5. Where did he live when he first came to the United States?
6. Where else has he lived?
7. How many times has he moved?
8. Where is he living now?
9. How long has he lived there?
10. How many degrees has he earned?
11. When did he get his B.S.? His M.S.?
12. After he got his B.S., how long did it take him to get his M.S.?
13. How many colleges has he attended?
14. What was his major field in college?
15. What is his occupation now?
16. How long has he been in the U.S.A.?
17. How old is he?

**B. Write both the questions and answers about Dr. Minton's life. The first question is written for you. Use complete sentences and write on your own paper.**

1. Where/born? *Where was she born?*
2. When/born?
3. How old/now?
4. Has/ever/be/USA?
5. How many degrees/have?
6. When/get/BA? MA? PhD?
7. Where/get/BA?
8. What//major/university?
9. How many universities/attend?
10. How old/get/PhD?
11. What/occupation now?
12. Where/work?
13. How long/be/psychologist?
14. How long ago/get/BA?
15. When/be/married?
16. How long/be/married?

**Skill Objectives: Interpreting a chart; reviewing verb tenses; answering and writing questions.** Examine the chart as a class. If needed, explain the abbreviated dates and the meaning and pronunciation of the degree titles. Adjust the amount of preliminary discussion to the needs of your class, then assign the page as independent work. Extension Activities: 1) Have the class discuss ways in which Amin Jabbour and Isabel Minton are alike, and ways in which they are different. 2) Have students write a short biography of Amin or Isabel based on the information in the chart.

## Dear Dot

Dear Dot—

My girlfriend Karen has broken several dates with me recently.
She calls me on the day of our date and says that she can't make
it. Sometimes she explains, but most times she doesn't. Last week
I drove to her apartment and I found a note on her door. It said
that she was at her sister's house. I called the number she put in
the note, but there was no answer. I have talked to Karen about
this situation. She says that she still loves me, and that if I am
patient, everything is going to be all right. I am trying to be
patient, but I am getting tired of her canceling our dates. What's
your opinion, Dot? What should I do?

Ted

1. What has happened to Ted recently? _____

_____

2. Does Karen explain when she breaks a date? _____

_____

3. What happened last week? _____

_____

4. Where did Karen say she was going to be? _____

_____

5. What is Ted getting tired of? _____

_____

6. What does the word *canceling* mean in this letter? Circle the best answer.

   a. calling about     b. calling for     c. calling off     d. calling in

7. What is your advice to Ted? Discuss your answer in class. Then write Ted a letter telling him
   what you think he should do and should not do.

   _____ ,

   _____

   _____

   _____

   _____

   _____

   _____

   _____

**Skill Objectives: Reading for details; drawing conclusions; making judgments; writing a letter.** Have students read the letter and
answer questions 1-6 independently. Correct these as a class. Then have students discuss question 7 and write their letters. Ask several volunteers
to read their letters, and have the class make suggestions for rephrasing, etc. As an additional option, you may wish to have students write a letter
from Karen to Ted explaining what she has been doing for the last six weeks and why she hasn't been able to see him.

101

# Which Tense?

Use sentence context to choose the right verb tense.

Read the sentences and decide whether to use the:

| | | |
|---|---|---|
| **Simple Present** | **Simple Past** | **Future** |
| **Present Progressive** | **Past Progressive** | **Present Perfect** |

Then write the verb in the blank using the correct form of the tense you chose. The first one is done for you.

1. Roberto _____*has been*_____ (be) to New York three times.

2. Sometimes we _____ (play) cards on Friday nights.

3. Kathy and Mike are living in Chicago where they _____ (live) for six years.

4. The children _____ (play) outside when the fire started.

5. I _____ (study) French from 1987 to 1988.

6. The mail never _____ (come) on Sundays.

7. Trang _____ (graduate) from college next June.

8. We _____ (stay) at the Biltmore Hotel for a few days last year.

9. Paul Theroux _____ (write) 25 books since 1970.

10. When you _____ (call) me yesterday, I _____ (type) a term paper.

11. My grandmother _____ (take) two night courses at the community college this semester.

12. Mae Ling _____ (be) ten on her next birthday.

13. It _____ (rain) now. It _____ (rain) for two days.

14. Listen! I think someone _____ (knock) at the door right now.

15. Ron and Jennifer usually _____ (go) to church on Sundays.

16. The Carlsson family _____ (move) three times since they arrived in this country.

17. A dog _____ (bite) John while he _____ (wait) for the bus last week.

18. How much was that sweater?

    It _____ (cost) $30.00.

19. Where is your sister?

    She _____ (shop).

20. The bus _____ (come) in a few minutes.

**Skill Objective: Reviewing all tenses taught to this point.** This page can be used as a quiz, with minimum explanation required, just enough to be sure that students understand the task. It can also be used as review and reinforcement, in which case you will wish to do the first few sentences together before assigning the page as independent work.

# Word Skills: Categories

A good way to test your word knowledge is to complete categories of words. A category is a group of similar things, in this case words. **After each category name below, write five words that belong in the category. Use any words that fit the category name. Use your dictionary or other books if you need to.** The first one is done for you.

1. Colors     _red_     _orange_     _green_     _blue_     _yellow_

2. Clothing

3. Vegetables

4. Fruit

5. Cities

6. States

7. Countries

8. School Subjects

9. Large Animals

10. Small Animals

11. Months

12. Sports

13. Occupations

14. Family Members

15. Machines

16. Rooms in a House

17. Kinds of Buildings

18. Weather Words

19. Motor Vehicles

20. Illnesses

---

# Here To Stay (2)

**A. Make sure you know the meaning of the following important words which are underlined in the story.**

| | | | | |
|---|---|---|---|---|
| led | admiral | claimed | mission | crowds |
| briefly | buccaneer | priests | provided | fortune |

**B. Read the story quickly to get some general ideas about it. Then read it again more slowly to answer the questions.**

## The West Coast

Juan Cabrillo Rodriguez was the first European to explore California. In 1542, he led a group of Spanish sailors from Mexico up the Pacific coast of North America. They explored about 75 miles of the California coast. They stopped briefly at present-day San Diego, but they did not settle in California. The sailors returned to Mexico.

The next important visitor to California was the English admiral and buccaneer, Sir Francis Drake. In 1579, Drake landed on the California coast and explored the land near what is now San Francisco. Drake claimed the entire northwest coast of North America for England. Neither he nor his men stayed to live on the land. They left North America to the Indians who were already living there.

It wasn't until 1769 that the first Europeans began to live in California. Father Junipero Serra and other Spanish priests started the first mission in San Diego in that year. After the Mexican Revolution in 1823, California officially became part of Mexico. By 1846, there were 21 missions along the coast of California. The missions stretched from San Diego to San Francisco. They provided training and education for the Indians. By 1846, however, large ranch owners took over the missions.

In that year, Mexico and the United States went to war. At the end of the war, California became a part of the United States. The priests returned to Mexico, and American settlers moved into California.

In 1848, a man named James Marshall found gold at John Sutter's mill, near present-day Sacramento. At first, no one paid attention to the discovery, but by 1849, crowds of people were coming to find their fortunes. In the four years after the discovery of gold, the population of California grew from 15,000 to 250,000! Soon, settlers were moving north to what today we call the states of Oregon and Washington. The new settlers came from the East to live on this land. They worked hard to build new lives for themselves. They didn't want to go back East. Like the first settlers of Plymouth and Jamestown, they were here to stay.

**C. Think carefully and answer the following question.**

You can conclude from the reading that California became a part of the United States because

a. Marshall discovered gold there in 1848.
b. Francis Drake declared California an English-speaking territory.
c. the Jamestown settlers moved to California.
d. Mexico lost the war and had to give up some of its territory.

*(Go on to the next page.)*

**Skill Objectives: Reading comprehension; drawing conclusions; building vocabulary.** Review the directions with the students. After the first reading, you may want to lead a discussion about the meaning of the highlighted vocabulary words. Encourage students to check and refine their definitions by using a dictionary. Display a U.S. and world map. Have students locate the places mentioned in the reading.

**D. What is this story mostly about? Circle your answer.**

a. the discovery of gold in California
b. the California coast
c. the early history of California
d. the American Indians in California

**E. Use a word from the underlined vocabulary to complete each of these sentences.**

1. Mr. Chin won a _____ in the lottery last week.

2. There were _____ of people at the airport to see the stars.

3. Janet was in a hurry, so we spoke only _____.

4. There were several _____ at the church last week.

5. The general _____ his troops into battle and won.

**F. Number the statements in the order in which they happened in the story.** The number 1 is done for you.

_____ California became a part of the United States.

___1___ Juan Cabrillo Rodriguez led Spanish sailors up the coast of California.

_____ Father Junipero Serra began the California missions.

_____ Drake claimed all of the Northwest for England.

_____ California became part of Mexico.

_____ The Mexican-American war began.

_____ Sir Francis Drake landed in California.

_____ People came west to look for gold.

_____ James Marshall found gold at Sutter's mill.

**G. Draw a line from each quotation at the left to the name of the most likely speaker.**

1. "The Indians need our help. We can teach them our language, our religion, and our culture at the missions."

2. "Gold! I've found gold!"

3. "There are people all over my property looking for gold."

4. "I claim this land for Her Majesty Queen Elizabeth."

5. "Back to the ships, men, and we sail back south. We've seen all there is to see here."

a. Juan Cabrillo Rodriguez
b. Sir Francis Drake
c. Father Junipero Serra
d. John Sutter
e. James Marshall

# Crossword Puzzle

Use irregular past tense verbs to solve the puzzle.

**Write the words in the right places.** Number 1 Across and number 1 Down are done for you.

## Across

1. what they did at the beach
4. battled
6. operated the car
7. what they did with the milk
10. kept out of sight
11. looked at or watched
12. I _____, I saw, I conquered.
13. didn't win
15. what the wind did
17. discovered
19. what the thief did
20. what the bicyclist did
21. mailed the letter
22. received
23. listened
26. constructed
28. said

## Down

1. what the singers did
2. she _____ her bed
3. smashed the glass
4. what the pilot did
5. same as 23 across
8. was aware of
9. donated
10. She _____ the baby in her arms.
12. selected
14. wondered
15. She _____ home the bacon.
16. He _____ his new suit.
18. didn't give away
19. didn't stand
24. what the diners did
25. He _____ his homework.
26. what the mad dog did
27. what the front person did

(Answers on page 125)

**Skill Objective: Reviewing past tense of irregular verbs.** Solve the first across and down clues as a class. Be sure students understand how to fill in a crossword puzzle. Students may work on this puzzle individually or in pairs. Students can check their spelling by referring to the verb list on page 122.

# Two Couples

**A. Read the story. Then answer the questions. Use complete sentences.** The first one is done for you.

Hop Nguyen came to Canton, Ohio, from Vietnam with her husband, Vuong, in 1978. When they first came, Vuong found a job in a Chinese restaurant. He worked there for only one year, because he found a better job with a computer company, where he still works today. Hop also found a job when she first came. She worked in a day-care center. When she first started there, she was a day-care worker, but now she is the manager. Both Hop and Vuong went to English classes when they first arrived, but now they study English only one night a week at the Adult Education Center.

1. When did Hop and Vuong come to the United States? _____ *They came to* _____ *the United States in 1978.*

2. Where did Vuong work when he first came? _____

3. In what year did he start to work for a computer company? _____

4. How long has he been working at the computer company? _____

5. When did Hop first find a job? _____

6. Is she working for the day-care center now? _____

7. How long has she been working there? _____

8. When did Hop and Vuong begin to study English? _____

9. How long have they been studying English? _____

10. How long have they been in the United States? _____

**B. Read the story about Jose and Daysi. On your paper, write questions like the ones about Hop and Vuong. Then write answers to the questions. You may wish to exchange papers with a partner and answer each other's questions.**

Jose Rodriguez came to Dallas in 1970. He started to work at the bank at that time. A year later he bought a car, and in 1972 he was married to Daysi Ayala. In 1974, Jose and Daysi bought a house, and in 1975, their first child, Maria Elena, was born.

Today, Jose and Daysi still live in Dallas. Jose still works at the same bank, still drives the same car, and still lives in the same house. But today Jose and Daysi have three children.

# Stormy Weather!

**A. Make sure you know the meaning of the following important words which are under-lined in the story.**

| | | | |
|---|---|---|---|
| meteorologists | hurricane | occur | snowdrifts |
| define | tornado | blizzards | sleet |
| dangerous | damage | cloudbursts | hail |

**B. Read the story quickly to get some general ideas about it. Then read it again more slowly to answer the questions.**

## Weather

Bad weather is like bad news; it comes in many forms. When most people think of bad weather, they think of rain and snow. There are many kinds of bad weather, however. Meteorologists, people who study weather, have named and defined all of the different kinds of bad weather.

Perhaps the most dangerous weather situations are hurricanes and tornadoes. A hurricane is a great wind-storm that covers hundreds of square miles for as long as 24 hours at a time. A hurricane brings along a lot of rain as well as very strong winds. Hurricanes can do millions of dollars worth of damage to property. Hurricanes occur most often in the summertime.

A tornado is a whirling windstorm. It doesn't have the rain of a hurricane but it moves very fast and does a lot of damage. Tornadoes have destroyed whole towns in the midwestern part of the United States. In 1925, in the southern central part of the United States, 689 people were killed by a tornado that lasted only three hours. Because they look like great twisted ropes of cloud, tornadoes are often called "twisters."

Blizzards and cloudbursts aren't as dangerous as hurricanes and tornadoes, but they are certainly bad weather. A cloudburst is a very heavy rainstorm that falls for a short period of time. The record for a cloudburst is one and a half inches of rain in one minute in Guadeloupe in the Caribbean. A blizzard is a snowstorm with a strong wind. The strong winds of a blizzard blow the snow everywhere. Driving a car becomes very dangerous, because you cannot see anything in front of you. The hills of snow, called snowdrifts, can block roads and trap people inside their houses for days.

Hailstorms and sleet storms are other bad weather situations. Hail is made of balls of ice, called hailstones. Hail forms when raindrops freeze high in the sky. When it hails, people run for protection. The icy balls can really hurt! Sleet is rain that freezes as it falls. Sleet isn't as large as hail and doesn't hurt as much as hail, but it is best to stay inside during either of these storms.

You can hear all these words if you watch the national weather reports on network television news programs. Weather forecasters on these programs tell about weather all over the country. Tune in several evenings and you'll hear all about weather!

**C. Think carefully and answer the following question.**

According to the reading, what other condition can you be sure of if you hear there is a tornado?

a. It's not raining.      b. It's summer.

c. It's hot.              d. It's the South.

(Go on to the next page.)

**Skill Objectives: Reading comprehension; building vocabulary.** Review the directions with the students. After the first reading, you may want to lead a discussion about the meaning of the highlighted vocabulary words. Encourage students to check and refine their definitions by using a dictionary.

**D. Circle the answer that best completes the sentence.**

A hurricane is different from a tornado because

a. it carries fast winds.
b. it happens in the United States.
c. it causes a lot of damage.
d. it brings a lot of rain.

**E. Use a word from the underlined vocabulary to complete each of these sentences.**

1. It is _____ to drive faster than the speed limit.

2. The accident caused a lot of _____ to Helen's van.

3. Miguel's father is a _____ at the television station.

4. It is difficult to _____ the word "weather."

5. Small earthquakes _____ every day somewhere in the world.

**F. Use separate paper to write answers to these questions.**

1. What is a meteorologist?
2. What is a hurricane?
3. What is a tornado?
4. Where have tornadoes done a lot of damage?
5. What is a cloudburst?
6. What is a blizzard?
7. Why is it dangerous to drive in a blizzard?
8. What is a snowdrift?
9. What is hail?
10. What is sleet?

**G.** Weather maps are issued by the National Weather Service every day. They show the weather in different parts of the country. This map shows the midcontinental United States one February day. **Look at the key at the top of the map and answer these questions.**

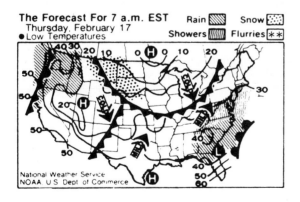

1. What is the weather like in the northwest part of the country? _____

2. What is the weather like in the Southeast? _____

3. Is it snowing anywhere? If so, where? _____

4. The numbers stand for temperatures. What part of the country is very cold? _____

5. What part of the country is quite warm? _____

**H. Use an encyclopedia to find out what the other symbols on the weather map mean. Then write a paragraph on your paper telling as much as you can about the weather on this February day.**

**Skill Objectives: Reading for details; building vocabulary; drawing conclusions; interpreting and writing about a weather map.**
Assign Parts C–F as independent work. Display a map with state names to help students answer question G-3. If you wish, do Part G as a class.
Explain "isotherms," the lines connecting points of equal temperature, and the symbols for high and low pressure areas and warm and cold fronts.
Extensions: Collect weather maps from newspapers, listen to TV weather reports, and if possible, call local toll-free weather information.

## Dear Dot

Dear Dot—

My husband Jack is teaching our daughters to work with tools and fix things around the house—even the car. He says that nowadays girls have to be able to do things for themselves. I don't know how to fix the car or a sink or anything, for that matter, and to tell the truth, I really don't want to know. The girls seem to like doing the work, but I'm not sure if it is such a good idea. The other day I found them in the attic, trying to fix an old television set. I'm afraid that they could hurt themselves. What do you think? Should I put a stop to all this?

Old-Fashioned Mother

1. What is Jack doing for his daughters? _____

_____

2. Why is he doing this? _____

_____

3. How do the girls feel about their lessons? _____

_____

4. What is Old-Fashioned Mother afraid of? _____

_____

5. What does the word *seem* mean in this letter? Circle your answer.

    a. appear    b. need    c. looked    d. want

6. What do you think Old-Fashioned Mother should do? Discuss your answer in class. Then take Dot's role and write Old-Fashioned a letter giving her your advice.

    _____ ,

    _____

    _____

    _____

    _____

    _____

    _____

    _____

                                                       _____

**Skill Objectives: Reading for details; drawing conclusions; making judgments; writing a letter.** Have students read the letter and answer questions 1–5 independently. Correct these as a class. Then have students discuss question 6 and write their letters. Have several volunteers read their letters, and have the class make suggestions for rephrasing, etc. As an additional option, have each student write about something he or she does well—making scrambled eggs, changing a tire, painting a room, for example. The student should write clear directions for the activity, as if they were for someone who has never done the activity before.

# Comparisons With Adjectives

**Look at the rules for writing the comparative form of adjectives.**

1. For one-syllable adjectives: add *-er* and *than.*

   | large | larger than | New York is *larger than* Chicago. |
   | fast | faster than | A car is *faster than* a bicycle. |

2. For two-syllable adjectives that end in *y*: change *y* to *i*, add *-er* and *than.*

   | easy | easier than | Math is *easier than* physics. |
   | pretty | prettier than | Your dress is *prettier than* mine. |

3. For other adjectives of two or more syllables: use *more ---- than.*

   | famous | famous than | Stevie Wonder is *more famous than* Ray Charles. |
   | expensive | more expensive than | Steak is *more expensive than* chicken. |

4. Irregular adjectives

   | good | better than | Tea is *better than* coffee, I think. |
   | bad | worse than | My English is *worse than* yours. |

**A.** **Add *-er* or *more ---- than* to the following words. Use the rules to help you.** The first two are done for you.

1. big _____*bigger than*_____
2. pretty _____*prettier than*_____
3. good _____
4. boring _____
5. small _____
6. important _____
7. nice _____
8. valuable _____

9. warm _____
10. intelligent _____
11. popular _____
12. noisy _____
13. great _____
14. smart _____
15. expensive _____
16. poor _____

**B.** **Write the correct form of the comparative in the sentences below.** The first one is done for you.

1. The Nile River is _____*longer than*_____ (long) the Amazon River.
2. People are _____ (intelligent) animals.
3. Florida is _____ (sunny) Michigan.
4. Boston is _____ (small) New York City.
5. I think that history is _____ (interesting) algebra.
6. Chicago is _____ (cold) Miami.
7. A Ford is _____ (economical) a Mercedes.
8. A Toyota is _____ (cheap) a Cadillac.
9. Dogs are _____ (friendly) cats.
10. I think that chicken is _____ (good) fish.

**Skill Objective: Learning rules for forming comparatives.** Review the rules with the class and write additional examples on the board. *Part A:* Show how the two examples follow rules 1 and 2. Then assign the rest of Part A. *Part B:* Be sure students understand the use of the adjective in parentheses: *(long)* is the word that is to be written in the comparative form. Assign Part B for independent work.

**111**

# Superlatives With Adjectives

**Look at the rules for writing the superlative form of adjectives.**

| | | |
|---|---|---|
| 1. For one-syllable adjectives: use *the ----est.* | | |
| large | the largest | Mexico City is *the largest* city in the world. |
| tall | the tallest | The Sears building is *the tallest* building. |
| 2. For two-syllable adjectives that end in *y:* change *y* to *i*, use *the ----est.* | | |
| pretty | the prettiest | Sue is *the prettiest* girl in the class. |
| funny | the funniest | Jose is *the funniest* person I know. |
| 3. For two or more syllables: use *the most ----.* | | |
| beautiful | the most beautiful | I think Paris is *the most beautiful* city. |
| handsome | the most handsome | Bob is *the most handsome* boy in our club. |
| 4. Irregular adjectives | | |
| good | the best | Kim is *the best* student in my class. |
| bad | the worst | "Jim's Diner" is *the worst* restaurant in town. |

**A.** **Add ----est or *the most ----* to the following words. Use the rules to help you. The first two are done for you.**

1. famous *the most famous*
2. large *the largest*
3. rich _____
4. heavy _____
5. honest _____
6. modern _____
7. strong _____
8. powerful _____

9. bad _____
10. lazy _____
11. economical _____
12. exciting _____
13. ugly _____
14. straight _____
15. cheap _____
16. interesting _____

**B.** **Write the correct form of the superlative in the sentences below.** The first one is done for you.

1. Mt. Everest is _____ *the highest* _____ (high) mountain in the world.

2. Queen Elizabeth II is _____ (rich) woman in the world.

3. John F. Kennedy was _____ (young) president of the U.S.

4. *The New York Times* is _____ (important) newspaper in New York.

5. Bennington College was _____ (expensive) college in the United States in 1988.

6. Mohammed Ali is probably _____ (famous) boxer in the U.S.

7. _____ (old) university in the world is in Morocco.

8. Many Americans think that Abraham Lincoln was _____ (great) U.S. president.

**112**

**Skill Objective: Learning rules for forming superlatives.** Review the rules with the class and write additional examples on the board. *Part A:* Show how the two examples follow rules 3 and 1. Then assign the rest of Part A. *Part B:* Be sure students understand how to complete the sentences, then assign Part B as independent work.

# Fact or Opinion?

You remember that a fact is a generally accepted statement of truth that can be checked in a dictionary, encyclopedia, or other reference book. An opinion, on the other hand, expresses a personal feeling, idea, or point of view.

**Read the following statements. Decide if each is a fact or an opinion. If it is a fact, circle the F; if it is an opinion, circle the O.**

F   O    1. The United States is larger than Cuba.

F   O    2. Summer is the best season of the year.

F   O    3. California is prettier than New York.

F   O    4. St. Augustine is the oldest city on the United States mainland.

F   O    5. The Rocky Mountains are higher than the Appalachians.

F   O    6. Movies are more interesting than television programs.

F   O    7. Spanish is more difficult to learn than French.

F   O    8. Puppies are the cutest of all baby animals.

F   O    9. Alaska is the largest of the fifty states.

F   O   10. The Pacific Ocean is the largest of the four oceans.

F   O   11. Apples are more delicious than oranges.

F   O   12. Fresh fruit is more nutritious than potato chips.

F   O   13. The Nile is the longest river in the world.

F   O   14. Paris is the most interesting city in Europe.

F   O   15. The moon is the earth's closest neighbor in the sky.

F   O   16. China has the largest population of any country in the world.

F   O   17. Hurricanes occur most often in the summer.

F   O   18. George Washington was the best United States President.

F   O   19. Cancer is the worst disease that a person can have.

F   O   20. Christopher Columbus crossed the ocean in 1492.

F   O   21. The atom is a very small particle of matter.

F   O   22. The Declaration of Independence is a radical document.

F   O   23. Liver is richer in vitamin B than eggs.

F   O   24. The sun is farther away from the earth than is Mars.

F   O   25. The American colonists were right to revolt against the British.

F   O   26. Thomas Edison was the greatest American inventor.

F   O   27. Train travel is more comfortable than plane travel.

F   O   28. There is no life as we know it on the moon.

F   O   29. Democracy is the best form of government.

F   O   30. Gold is more expensive than silver.

# Make Some Comparisons

**A. Compare a car and a bicycle. Use the adjectives in the box in their proper form. Write as many sentences as you can.** One is written for you.

| | | | | | | |
|---|---|---|---|---|---|---|
| big | expensive | fast | safe | noisy | easy to park | economical |
| relaxing | healthy | | heavy | cold in the winter | | comfortable |
| exciting to drive or ride | | | | dangerous | | easy to fix |

1. *A car is bigger than a bicycle.*

2. _____

3. _____

4. _____

5. _____

6. _____

7. _____

8. _____

9. _____

10. _____

11. _____

12. _____

**B. Study the chart with the three cars and then look at the adjectives below it. On your paper write a paragraph comparing the three cars. Use comparatives and superlatives of the adjectives.**

| **BMW** | **CADILLAC** | **HONDA** |
|---|---|---|
| Price: $48,000 | $28,000 | $13,000 |
| MPG: 28 miles per gal. | 18 miles per gal. | 35 miles per gal. |
| MPH: 100 miles per hr. | 120 miles per hr. | 95 miles per hr. |
| Number of cylinders: 6 | 8 cylinders | 4 cylinders |
| Automatic Shift | 4 speed shift | 5 speed shift |
| Seats 5 people | Seats 6 people | Seats 4 people |

| | | | |
|---|---|---|---|
| easy to drive | slow | comfortable | fast |
| easy to park | small (size) | powerful | |
| economical (gasoline) | small (engine) | cheap | |

For example: The BMW is *the most expensive.* The Honda is *cheaper than* the Cadillac.

**Skill Objectives: Writing sentences with comparatives; interpreting a chart.** *Part A:* Go over the directions with the class. Do a few sentences on the board together before assigning Part A as independent work. *Part B:* Have pairs of students make the comparisons orally before you assign Part B as independent work.

# Vacation Time

Travel is big business. Hotels, airlines, and travel agents advertise in newspapers and magazines to attract visitors to vacation spots. Here are three advertisements. **Complete them with appropriate words.** The first one is done for you. **Use comparatives in the second advertisement and superlatives in the third.**

COME TO BEAUTIFUL BERMUDA!

The beaches are ___clean___ and ___white___ !

The weather is ___warm___ and ___sunny___ !

The people are ___friendly___ !

The hotels are ___modern___ !

The food is ___delicious___ !

The discos are ___exciting___ and ___cheap___ !

Yes, come to Bermuda, and you'll have a ___great___ time!

ONLY $399!
HOTEL & AIR FARE

COME TO ROMANTIC ARUBA!

The beaches are ___cleaner___ and ___whiter___ !

The weather is _____ and _____ !

The people are _____ !

The hotels are _____ !

The food is _____ !

The rooms are _____ and _____ !

Yes, come to Aruba, and you'll have a _____ time!

ONLY $299!
HOTEL & AIR FARE

COME TO SUPER ST. THOMAS!

The beaches are ___the cleanest___ and ___whitest___ !

The weather is _____ and _____ !

The people are _____ !

The hotels are _____ !

The food is _____ !

The rooms are _____ and _____ !

Yes, come to St. Thomas and you'll have _____ time!

ONLY $199!
HOTEL & AIR FARE

# More Vacation Time

Words with more than two syllables usually do not use *er* and *est* to form the comparative and superlative. Instead, they use the words *more* and *the most*. The comparative of *exciting* is *more exciting*. The superlative is *the most exciting*. **Use this rule in helping you write advertisements for these three ski vacation sports. Use comparatives and superlatives in your ads.**

COME TO THE MOUNTAINS
OF MONTANA!

_____

$399.00
HOTEL & AIR
ONE WEEK!

High mountains
Beautiful snow
Cool, clear days
Lift tickets
$15/day
Good discos
Interesting
people

COME TO THE WHITE MOUNTAINS
OF NEW HAMPSHIRE!

_____

$350.00
HOTEL & AIR
ONE WEEK!

High mountains
Beautiful snow
Cool, clear days
Lift tickets
$12/day
Good discos
Interesting
people

COME TO THE COLORADO ROCKIES!

_____

$299.00
HOTEL & AIR
ONE WEEK!

High mountains
Beautiful snow
Cool, clear days
Lift tickets
$10/day
Good discos
Interesting
people

**Skill Objectives: Constructing comparatives and superlatives; using *more* and *the most*.** Write the first travel ad as a class, using the information in the ad and following the style set on page 115: *The mountains are high. The snow is beautiful. . . . The lift tickets are cheap, etc.* You may wish to have the class compose the other two ads orally before assigning the page as independent work. Extension Activity: Have students write a travel ad, using superlatives to describe their school, town, favorite store, or native country.

116

# The Sunshine State

Answer true/false/? items about Florida, and write your ideas.

Florida is a middle-sized state. It is a peninsula in the southeastern United States, and has the longest ocean coastline of any state. The city of Key West is the southernmost city in the United States. Florida is the second fastest growing state. Only California is growing faster.

Florida is a famous resort state, because the climate is warm in the winter, the beaches are beautiful, and the fishing is excellent. The most popular resort cities on the east coast are Miami Beach and Palm Beach. On the west coast, St. Petersburg and Tampa are popular. St. Augustine, in the northern part of the state, is the oldest city on the United States mainland. It was founded in 1565.

Orlando is the city where Walt Disney World and the Epcot Center are located. About 40,000 tourists visit Disney World every day. The Orlando airport is a very busy place—almost as busy as Miami's airport, which is one of the busiest in the country. Cape Canaveral, about forty miles east of Orlando, is often in the news because it is a test center for satellites, missiles, the space shuttle, and other United States spaceships.

Many of the people in Florida make their living from the tourist trade, but fruit raising and farming are also important; and there is a large fishing industry. Oranges, grapefruit, and other citrus fruit grow across central Florida from the Atlantic Ocean to the Gulf of Mexico. Frozen orange juice is one of Florida's most important products.

**A. Read the statements below. If the statement is true, write *T*. If the statement is false, write *F*. If the story doesn't give you enough information to know if the statement is true or false, write *?*.** The first two are done for you.

_F_ 1. Florida is located in the southwestern United States.

_?_ 2. A lot of retired people live in Florida.

_____ 3. Florida is growing as fast as California.

_____ 4. Key West is the southernmost city in the United States.

_____ 5. Florida is famous for its climate, beaches, and fishing.

_____ 6. Most people move to Florida because of the beautiful beaches.

_____ 7. Popular East Coast beaches are Tampa and Miami.

_____ 8. The oldest city on the United States mainland is located in Florida.

_____ 9. More people visit Disney World than the Epcot Center.

_____ 10. The Epcot Center is designed for adults.

_____ 11. Cape Canaveral is a famous space center.

_____ 12. Frozen orange juice is Florida's leading industry.

_____ 13. Miami has two major airports.

_____ 14. Florida has 40,000 tourists every day.

_____ 15. Farming and fishing are important industries in Florida.

**B. On your own paper, write why you would or would not like to live in Florida. If you live there now, tell why you like or dislike it.**

Skill Objectives: Reading for details; distinguishing between *true, false,* and *?*. *Part A:* Go over any new vocabulary, and find out what the students already know about Florida. Then have students read the article silently. Review the *T, F, ?* format; make sure students understand that the *?* response is used when the story doesn't give enough information to decide if the statement is true or false. (Some students may know from outside reading or personal experience that a statement is true or not true, but still should use the *?* response if this information is not in the story.)

# Biggest, Largest, Longest!

**A. Make sure you know the meaning of the following important words which are underlined in the story.**

| | | | | |
|---|---|---|---|---|
| whale | ton | tortoise | falcon | leopard |
| weigh | insect | ostrich | cheetah | penny |

**B. Read the story quickly to get some general ideas about it. Then read it again more slowly to answer the questions.**

## Animal Champions

Zoologists, scientists who study animals, tell us the following facts about animals:

- The blue whale is the largest animal in the world. It can be 100 feet long and can weigh more than 100 tons.
- The longest insect is the walking stick. It can be up to 16 inches long.
- The largest fish is the shark. (Remember, a whale is not a fish; it is a mammal.) Sharks can be 45 feet long.
- The giant tortoise of South America has the longest life of any animal. These turtles can live to be 150 years old.
- The ostrich is the largest bird. Ostriches can be 8 feet tall. They can weigh 200 pounds.
- The fastest bird is the peregrine falcon. It can fly at speeds of more than 217 miles per hour.
- The fastest runner is the cheetah. This hunting leopard can run at speeds of 60 miles per hour.
- The tallest animal is the giraffe. Some giraffes are 19 feet tall.
- The anaconda is the longest and heaviest snake. It can be 37 feet long and weigh more than 250 pounds.
- Hummingbirds are the smallest birds. An adult hummingbird can weigh less than a penny.
- The largest animal on land is the African elephant. It can weigh more than 6 tons.

**C. Think carefully and answer the following question.**

According to the article, which of the following could possibly live for more than a century?

a. cheetah     b. tortoise     c. anaconda snake     d. elephant

**D. Use a word from the underlined vocabulary to complete each of these sentences.**

1. Those bricks _____ five pounds each.

2. I have a nickel, two dimes, a quarter, and a _____ .

3. Troy is scared of any bug or _____ .

4. The _____ is the largest animal in the sea.

5. Jean is as slow as an old _____ .

(Go on to the next page.)

**Skill Objectives: Reading comprehension; restating information; building vocabulary.** Review the directions with the students. After the first reading, you may want to lead a discussion about the meaning of the highlighted vocabulary words. Encourage students to check and refine their definitions by using a dictionary. Assign Part C as independent work.

**E.** **Decide whether each of these statements is true or false. If it is true, write *T.* If it is false, write *F.* If the story doesn't give you enough information to decide, write ?**

_____ 1. A whale is larger than a shark.

_____ 2. A cheetah is faster than a peregrine falcon.

_____ 3. The most dangerous animal is the leopard.

_____ 4. An ostrich is taller than a giraffe.

_____ 5. A walking stick is a kind of bird.

_____ 6. The most intelligent animal is the whale.

_____ 7. An anaconda is a long and heavy insect.

_____ 8. Blue whales are larger than African elephants.

_____ 9. Zoologists are scientists who study animals.

_____ 10. The smallest animal on earth is the hummingbird.

**F.** **Decide which class each of the following animals belongs to. Use the following classes: fish, amphibians, birds, reptiles, insects, and mammals. Use a dictionary or an encyclopedia if you are not sure.** The first one is done for you.

| | | | | |
|---|---|---|---|---|
| 1. eagle | _bird_ | 11. frog | _____ |
| 2. monkey | _____ | 12. crocodile | _____ |
| 3. shark | _____ | 13. grasshopper | _____ |
| 4. lion | _____ | 14. starling | _____ |
| 5. snake | _____ | 15. whale | _____ |
| 6. flea | _____ | 16. auk | _____ |
| 7. eel | _____ | 17. toad | _____ |
| 8. dragonfly | _____ | 18. bat | _____ |
| 9. sea horse | _____ | 19. kiwi | _____ |
| 10. minnow | _____ | 20. salamander | _____ |

**G.** **Find out about some other champions. Use an encyclopedia or other reference book if you need to. Use comparative and superlative forms of the adjective.** The first one is done for you. Use it as a model for the others.

1. Long Rivers of the World

Amazon _____longer_____

Chang (Yangtze) _____long_____

Nile _____longest_____

3. High Mountains of North America

McKinley _____

Orizaba (Citlaltepetl) _____

Logan _____

2. Big States in the United States

California _____

Alaska _____

Texas _____

4. Large Lakes of North America

Michigan _____

Superior _____

Huron _____

**Skill Objectives: Reading for details; drawing conclusions; classifying; building vocabulary.** Assign Parts C–E as independent work. You may wish to identify and discuss the characteristics of the six animal classes (fish, amphibians, birds, reptiles, insects, and mammals) with the group before assigning Part F as independent work. A World Almanac would be a good reference source for Part G.

**119**

## Dear Dot

Dear Dot—

I am heartbroken. My boyfriend Rafael just broke up with me. He said that he has a new girlfriend. He says that she is prettier, funnier, nicer, and more intelligent than I am. He always told me that I was the prettiest, funniest, nicest, and most intelligent girl in the world. How could he change his mind like that? I still love him. He is the most attractive and interesting boy I have ever dated. What can I do to get him back?

Lorna

1. Why is Lorna heartbroken? _____

_____

2. How does Rafael describe his new girlfriend? _____

_____

3. What did he used to tell Lorna? _____

_____

4. How does Lorna describe Rafael? _____

_____

5. What does the word *attractive* mean in this letter? Circle your answer.

a. bright     b. handsome     c. funny     d. frightening

6. What is your advice to Lorna? Discuss your answer in class, then write Dot's letter answering Lorna's question and telling her what you think she should do.

_____ ,

_____

_____

_____

_____

_____

_____

_____

_____

_____

_____

**Skill Objectives: Reading for details; drawing conclusions; making judgments; writing a letter.** Have students read the letter and answer questions 1–5 independently. Correct these as a class. Then have students discuss question 6 and write their letters. Have several volunteers read their letters to the class and have others offer comments and suggestions for rephrasing, etc. As an additional option, ask students to write a description of something that is the best—the best place they ever lived, the best meal they ever ate, etc. Have them tell why it was the best and why it was better than other things of the same kind.

**120**

# Verb Review: Past Tense (1)

Regular Verbs, present and past

## a. End with *d* sound

agree/agreed
allow/allowed
amuse/amused
answer/answered
apply/applied
arrive/arrived
call/called
carry/carried
change/changed
clean/cleaned
consider/considered
copy/copied
cry/cried
describe/described

die/died
discover/discovered
dry/dried
enjoy/enjoyed
enter/entered
fry/fried
hurry/hurried
learn/learned
listen/listened
live/lived
love/loved
improve/improved
marry/married

move/moved
order/ordered
prepare/prepared
remember/remembered
return/returned
save/saved
serve/served
stay/stayed
study/studied
travel/traveled
try/tried
use/used
worry/worried

## b. End with *t* sound

accomplish/accomplished
ask/asked
bake/baked
brush/brushed
chase/chased
cook/cooked
dress/dressed

finish/finished
increase/increased
look/looked
pack/packed
pick up/picked up
practice/practiced
miss/missed

talk/talked
type/typed
walk/walked
wash/washed
watch/watched
wax/waxed
work/worked

## c. End with sound of *id*

accept/accepted
attend/attended
collect/collected
complete/completed
correct/corrected
create/created

decide/decided
demand/demanded
insist/insisted
invent/invented
invite/invited
need/needed

paint/painted
recommend/recommended
start/started
suggest/suggested
visit/visited
want/wanted

NOTE: The past participles of regular verbs have the same form as the past tense. Example: *I study; I studied yesterday; I have studied all morning.*

**On your paper write twenty sentences using as many of the verbs on this list in the past tense as you can. Try to use two or three verbs in each sentence.** For example: *He was amused, but he agreed with me and allowed me to go.*

**Skill Objectives: Spelling and pronouncing regular past tense verbs; writing creative sentences.** Use as a review. Assign the writing exercise as optional independent work.

**121**

# Verb Review: Past Tense (2)

Irregular Verbs, present, past, and past participle

am, is, are/was, were/been

begin/began/begun
bite/bit/bitten
bleed/bled/bled
blow/blew/blown
break/broke/broken
bring/brought/brought
build/built/built
buy/bought/bought

catch/caught/caught
choose/chose/chosen
come/came/come
cost/cost/cost
cut/cut/cut

do/did/did
drink/drank/drunk
drive/drove/driven

eat/ate/eaten

fall/fell/fallen
feed/fed/fed
feel/felt/felt
fight/fought/fought
find/found/found
fit/fitted (or fit)/fitted(or fit)
fly/flew/flown
freeze/froze/frozen

get/got/gotten
give/gave/given
go/went/gone
grow/grew/grown

have/had/had
hear/heard/heard
hide/hid/hid (or hidden)
hit/hit/hit
hold/held/held

keep/kept/kept
know/knew/known

lead/led/led
leave/left/left
lose/lost/lost

make/made/made
meet/met/met

pay/paid/paid
put/put/put

read/read/read
ride/rode/ridden
ring/rang/rung
rise/rose/risen
run/ran/run

say/said/said
see/saw/seen
sell/sold/sold
send/sent/sent
set/set/set
sew/sewed/sewn
shake/shook/shaken
shoot/shot/shot
show/showed/shown
sing/sang/sung
sit/sat/sat
sleep/slept/slept
speak/spoke/spoken
spend/spent/spent
split/split/split
stand/stood/stood
steal/stole/stolen
swim/swam/swum

take/took/taken
teach/taught/taught
tell/told/told
think/thought/thought

understand/understood/
   understood

wake/woke (or waked)/
   waked (or woken)
wear/wore/worn
win/won/won
write/wrote/written

**On your paper write twenty sentences using as many of the verbs on this list in the past tense as you can. Try to use two or more verbs in each sentence. Then write twenty more sentences using the past participles of as many verbs as you can. Try to use different verbs from those you used in your past tense sentences.**

**Skill Objectives: Reviewing irregular verb forms, simple past tense and past participles; writing creative sentences.** Assign the writing exercise as optional independent work.

# End of Book Test: Completing Familiar Structures

**A. Circle the best answer.**

*Example:* John is _____ than his sister.

a. more old    (b. older)    c. more older    d. very older

1. Mary went to the library but her friends _____ go with her.

   a. weren't    b. aren't    c. don't    d. didn't

2. When did the plane arrive? It arrived _____.

   a. ten minutes ago    b. before ten minutes    c. in ten minutes    d. at ten minutes

3. Yesterday I _____ tired and stayed in bed.

   a. am    b. was    c. did    d. do

4. My friend _____ a new car.

   a. has    b. is having    c. have    d. is have

5. Cathy is _____ girl in the class.

   a. the most pretty    b. the prettiest    c. the more pretty    d. prettier than

6. I don't have much money but I have _____.

   a. little    b. a few    c. a little    d. few

7. Tom has been in the United States _____ 1978.

   a. for    b. until    c. after    d. since

8. How many times have you _____ the movie "Rocky"?

   a. see    b. saw    c. seeing    d. seen

9. I have _____ finished my homework.

   a. yet    b. been    c. already    d. until

10. Alexis is happy because he _____ a new car.

    a. has just bought    b. has bought yet    c. has boughten    d. has just buy

11. Bill _____ when I called him.

    a. was eating    b. ate    c. has eaten    d. is eating

12. Miami, Florida, is _____ than Boston.

    a. more warm    b. the warmest    c. warmer    d. more warmer

**End of Book Test: Completing familiar structures.** The following testing pages will help you evaluate each student's strengths and weaknesses and indicate his or her readiness to proceed to the next level of instruction. Review directions and examples with the class. *Part A:* Remind students to try each answer choice in the blank space to determine which choice is correct. Students should circle their answers.

**123**

# End of Book Test: Completing Familiar Structures (continued)

13. The teacher told me _____ more often.

    a. to study     b. study     c. studying     d. studies

14. Robert cut _____ when he was shaving.

    a. him     b. his     c. himself     d. he

15. When Mr. Stevens was young, he _____ play football very well.

    a. could     b. can     c. was     d. did

16. Mary likes _____.

    a. traveler     b. traveling     c. to traveling     d. traveled

17. There are _____ cookies in the kitchen.

    a. a little     b. a big     c. a few     d. a many

18. When Martha was young, she _____ wash the dishes every night.

    a. can     b. had to     c. was     d. have to

19. When I arrived, there wasn't _____ in the office.

    a. somebody     b. anybody     c. nobody     d. body

20. The police _____ the robber.

    a. catching     b. to catch     c. caught     d. were caught

21. Mrs. Smith _____ at the bank since 1980.

    a. worked     b. working     c. works     d. has worked

22. Ellen can't talk on the telephone now because she _____ her hair.

    a. was washing     b. wash     c. is washing     d. washes

23. Janet can't drive a car because she _____ a license.

    a. hasn't had     b. doesn't have     c. don't have     d. didn't have

24. I bought these gloves _____.

    a. in two weeks     b. for two weeks     c.  two weeks     d. two weeks ago

25. Dolores borrowed _____ books from the library.

    a. some     b. any     c. a little     d. much

**124**

# End of Book Test: Completing Familiar Structures (continued)

**B. Read each sentence. Write the correct form of the verb on the line.**

Examples: 1. Martha __went__ (go) to the bank yesterday.

2. Kenneth __goes__ (go) to the movies every day.

1. Tomorrow the hairdresser _____ (cut) my hair.

2. Last week George _____ (come) to class late.

3. My mother and father _____ (stay) at the Hilton Hotel now.

4. Linda _____ (work) at the bank many years ago.

5. John _____ (be) in the United States for ten years.

6. The President of the United States _____ (make) $200,000 a year.

7. When I arrived home, my mother _____ (make) lunch.

8. Harry and Larry _____ (see) the movie "Rocky" many times.

9. Paul _____ (sleep) at present.

10. My father _____ (get) up at six o'clock every morning.

## Answer to puzzle on page 106.

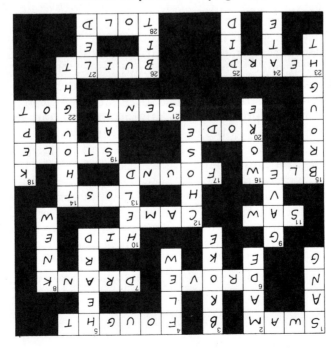

**End of Book Test: Completing familiar structures (continued).** *Part B:* Go over the directions and example with the class before assigning the page as independent work.

125

# End of Book Test: Reading Comprehension

## Sacajawea

One of the most interesting and colorful women in the early history of the United States is Sacajawea, the Shoshone Indian princess. When Sacajawea was young, Indians from another tribe, the Minnetaree, kidnapped her from her home in the Rocky Mountains. They brought her to live in the central plains, near the Missouri River. Sacajawea was twelve or thirteen when the Minnetaree kidnapped her, old enough so that she never forgot her Shoshone heritage.

When Sacajawea was seventeen years old, a French trader, Pierre Charboneau, took her for his wife. The Indian girl left the Minnetaree and lived up river with her French husband. Together they worked along the Missouri River, trading with the different Indian tribes.

In 1804, something happened to change their lives. Captain Meriwether Lewis and Captain William Clark came to the village where Charboneau and Sacajawea lived. The two captains explained to the couple that they were heading west. They said that they were looking for a guide to take them through the unknown central lands and across the Rocky Mountains.

Sacajawea was very excited. She knew that these men were going to the home of her family, the Shoshone Indians. Sacajawea agreed at once to be the guide for the captains and their men. But it was too late in the year to begin a long journey. The captains told Sacajawea that the trip wasn't going to begin until spring.

In February, Sacajawea had a baby. Some of the soldiers were afraid that Sacajawea was not going to be able to make the trip. But when the time came, there were no problems. Sacajawea was ready and able to march with the men. She put the baby, Pompe, on her back and marched easily with the others.

Sacajawea led the men across the plains. She helped them to communicate with the Indians they met. She led them up and into the great Rocky Mountains. All the time, however, Sacajawea was looking for members of her tribe. After many weeks in the mountains, her dreams came true. Sacajawea and the explorers found the Shoshone village. To her surprise, her brother Cameahwait was the new chief of the tribe. Sacajawea was happy; she was finally with her family once again.

The captains were glad that Sacajawea was with her family, but they needed a guide to help them finish their job. They asked Sacajawea to continue with them on their journey. To their delight, she agreed. She and her husband and the baby accompanied Captains Lewis and Clark on the rest of the trip. They continued through the mountains and across the Northwest. The explorers didn't stop until they reached the Pacific Ocean.

Finally the work of exploring and map-making was over. The explorers were ready to return home. When they reached the Rocky Mountains, there was a sad farewell. Sacajawea, her husband, and Pompe the baby were not returning to the East. They were going to stay with the Shoshone in the Rocky Mountains. The two captains asked the family to reconsider. They wanted them to meet President Thomas Jefferson, the man who had sent the explorers on the journey. Sacajawea refused. She didn't want to lose her family again.

Lewis and Clark never forgot Sacajawea. They knew that they owed much of their success to her. When the two explorers returned to the East, they wrote and spoke of her often. Sacajawea became one of the most famous women of the 1800s. Her name and fame still live today in American history.

(Go on to the next page.)

**End of Book Test: Reading comprehension.** Students should read the story several times before independently answering the comprehension questions on page 127. Encourage students to use context clues to guess the meanings of unfamiliar words. Dictionaries may also be used. The name of the heroine of this story is pronounced Sa kə jə wē' ə.

**A. Answer the following questions. Use complete sentences.**

1. Who kidnapped Sacajawea? _____

_____

2. Where did Lewis and Clark want to go? _____

_____

3. Why did Sacajawea want to go with Lewis and Clark? _____

_____

4. How did Sacajawea carry her baby on the long trip? _____

_____

5. Why didn't Sacajawea return to the East with Lewis and Clark? _____

_____

**B. Number these statements in the correct chronological order.**

_____ Pierre Charboneau married Sacajawea.

_____ Sacajawea found her family in the mountains.

_____ Lewis and Clark came to the village of Sacajawea and Charboneau.

_____ Sacajawea returned permanently to the Shoshone village.

_____ The Minnetaree captured Sacajawea.

_____ Sacajawea led the explorers through the Central Plains and into the Rocky Mountains.

_____ The explorers saw the Pacific Ocean.

_____ Sacajawea had a baby.

**C. Draw a conclusion to complete the sentence. Circle your answer.**

Lewis and Clark traveled through the West because

a. they were looking for gold.

b. they were looking for Sacajawea's family.

c. they were lost.

d. they were making maps of the new territory.

**D. Write the letter of the quotation next to the speaker's name.**

1. Sacajawea _____

2. Charboneau _____

3. Meriwether Lewis _____

4. Cameahwait _____

5. Thomas Jefferson _____

a. "My sister, how I have missed you all these years. I never expected to see you again."

b. "It is your job to explore this new territory and report back to me as soon as possible."

c. "I must return to the shining mountains, the land of my people."

d. "My partner and I need a guide to take us through the new land."

e. "You are a beautiful woman, and I want you to be my wife."

# Skills Index

The pages listed below are those on which the skills are introduced and/or emphasized. Many of the skills appear, incidentally, on other pages as well.